ALIVE AND KICKING

KICKING

THE ULTIMATE BOOK OF
'90s FOOTBALL
NOSTALGIA

ASH ROSE

First published 2013

The History Press
The Mill, Brimscombe Port
Stroud, Gloucestershire, GL5 2QG
www.thehistorypress.co.uk

British Library Cataloguing in Publication Data.
A catalogue record for this book is available from the British Library.

ISBN 978 0 7524 8273 6

Typesetting and origination by The History Press
Printed in India

CONTENTS

INTRODUCTION

My favourite word in the English language is nostalgia.

There are no bad connotations with the word, everyone likes to think back to a time in their life and get that warm fuzzy feeling in the pit of their stomach – whether it's about your loved ones, about the town and homes you lived in or the things you used to watch on the TV. For me, I get most nostalgic when I talk about the one thing I almost always talk about anyway – football, and specifically football in the 1990s.

Remember when your elders used to say that well-known clichéd phrase, 'It's not like the old days', and you'd think that will never be me saying that? Well, unfortunately over the last few years I've found myself using that exact same phrase when talking about modern day football. It's not that I don't like it, I love it and, in fact, in my day job all I do is write about and embrace the sport in 2013. However, at some point 1990s football suddenly became 'the old days'. Just look around you and see how many managers there are that you remember as players, or the birthdates of the new wave of English footballers; you'll realise somewhere down the road the 1990s stopped being a new era for English football and become a retro past that people like me (and hopefully you, seeing as you've picked up this book) now label as 'the good old days'. The generation has come full circle, already.

Now instead of worrying about this fact, and the tinge of grey hair that's started to shine through my brown locks, I decided it was time to embrace the era I still hold most dear to my heart. If the 1990s are now retro, then it needs a retro celebration of what made football, well ... football, in that memorable decade. I want to remember when videprinters and Teletext meant there was no need for Jeff Stelling on a Saturday, or when reaching an FA Cup final saw a whole day of television dedicated to the teams, and each recorded a ludicrous pop song to celebrate their achievement. I want to

switch on the TV and watch *Dream Team* or James Richardson on a Saturday morning discussing Italian football outside a Mediterranean café. Simply put, I want to feel like it is the 1990s all over again.

So sit back and enjoy a ride through a decade that will be remembered for players such as Cantona, Shearer and Owen, and World Cups that covered new continents, an era that changed the face of football thanks to the Premier League, Jean-Marc Bosman and Sky TV. This book celebrates all that, along with the TV shows, toys and video games we may or may not remember fondly. From Merlin stickers to classic kits, Gascoigne to Zidane, *Alive and Kicking* has football in the 1990s all wrapped up just for you, and well me too. Feeling nostalgic about the great game has never felt so good.

HERE'S TO THE NEW GOOD OLD DAYS.

Ash Rose

Just a little disclaimer, every effort has been made to show a variety of teams, but be aware that, as a QPR fan, most of the products are my own so they may appear more often than others. Blame my Dad for that one.

Here's hoping all the bases have been covered and your 1990s memory is included in these pages. Blame me if it's not.

1

ON THE PITCH

MITRE

If you were watching football in the 1990s, particularly at the beginning of the decade, then you were watching a Mitre football being kicked around a pitch. Established in 1817, they began supplying match day balls for the Football League in the late 1980s. At the beginning of the '90s (and before the Premier League) the ball used was called the Mitre Delta Max – famous for its v-shapes across the centre of the ball. These were also produced on the famous orange ball, which always got a cheer when it was rolled out on a snowy match day. Later came the Ultimax ball, which included the Premier League logo – this was the original microfibre ball and the first ever to be recorded moving at over 100mph. Mitre remained on Premier League pitches until 2000 when Nike took over the contract, however they continue to provide the Football League with balls to this day. It wasn't just balls either, Mitre were a name in the boot market too, most notably with the Pro Premier worn by players including Aston Villa striker Dean Saunders and Celtic stalwart Paul McStay.

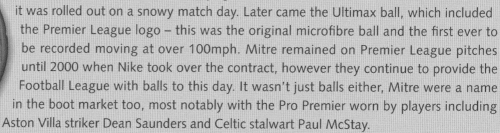

'90s MOMENT

The first ever Premier League goal was scored with the Mitre Ultimax when Brian Deane netted for Sheffield United against Manchester United in August 1992.

Mitre.
In a Different League

The big names in football are proud to be associated with the big name in sportswear.

World class players like Dean Saunders, Chris Waddle, Paul McStay and Steve Bruce depend on the quality of Mitre equipment to help them achieve peak performance.

That's why they trust Mitre's experience and choose to wear Mitre boots... And why the FA Premier League chose Mitre as the supplier of the official match ball.

The best quality boots, the finest footballs and the know-how nobody can compete with – that's the Mitre magic for players at every level, in every country.

It's been that way since long before the birth of organised League Football.

Try the Mitre experience for yourself and follow in the footsteps of the world's best.

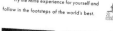

PRO MAX PREMIER LEAGUE FOOTBALL

PRO PREMIER FOOTBALL BOOTS

mitre
absolute performance

UMBRO

Umbro began the decade with the invention of laces on the Manchester United and Aston Villa kits, and ended it as suppliers of United's treble winning team. In between it saw a whole host of unforgettable kits and footwear, including full reign over the England football apparel. Shown here are some memorable catalogues from Umbro in the 1990s that include some of the decade's fashion disasters, both on and off the pitch. Some of their classic kits feature later in the book, but if there was ever a more 1990s statement than the tie-dyed products from the 1992 catalogue I haven't seen them – ah, it takes me back. 1994 saw Umbro deck out the World Cup winning Brazil team, while 1996 saw Umbro have a big influence on the Euro '96 tournament thanks to England's run, and David Seaman's goalie kit. Their most popular boot came in the form of the Speciali, worn by Alan Shearer throughout his career, and later Michael Owen.

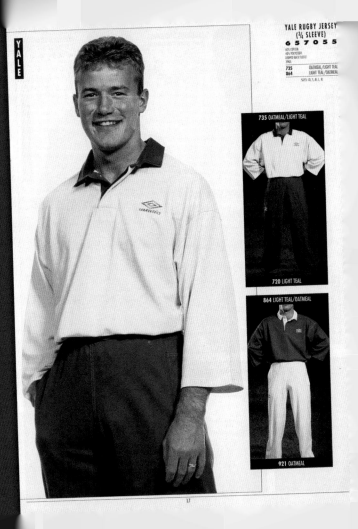

YALE

YALE RUGBY JERSEY
(¾ SLEEVE)
6 5 7 0 5 5

735   OATMEAL/LIGHT TEAL
864   LIGHT TEAL/OATMEAL

735 OATMEAL/LIGHT TEAL

720 LIGHT TEAL

864 LIGHT TEAL/OATMEAL

921 OATMEAL

'90S MOMENT

an Shearer made his
ngland debut in February
992, scoring in a 2–0 win
ver France. The game
arked the only time he
nd Gary Lineker shared
n England pitch.

TEES

Three new T-shirt designs have been
introduced for 92. The designs of England and
Scotland prints feature team colours, badge and
Umbro diamond. Also offered for 92 are a range of all over
print tees, in distinctive team colours.

ENGLAND

SCOTLAND

LICENSED OFFICIALLY PRODUCT

Our new boots have been out for 90 minutes.

After thoroughly testing our
new range of boots in the lab,
they're worn out. Out in the field.
By professionals like Alan Shearer
and Mark Hughes.

They field test them against
the rigours of a real match.
Checking for strength and comfort,
two properties derived from the
Whitblock Sole System. A bone in
the boot that acts just like the
bones in a foot.

All our top boots, the Special,
Supreme and
system. Along
They weigh so
metal ones, t
Special the m
As well as th
The design of
weight more
toughen it u

Finally,
totally happ
puts his com
why they're

The hea

1994 Catalog

UMBRO
the-boot you fe
at firstoutt.

ADIDAS

One word could sum up the Adidas effect on football in the 90s – Predator. It's the boot that changed the way boots were made, and is still one of the game's most popular pair of kickers. The brainchild of former Liverpool midfielder Craig Johnston, the Predator was launched in 1994. Dedicating his own time and money to the idea, the simple premise was to add rubber strips that Johnston used off a tennis ball to give a better grip and control on the ball. The design was taken on by Adidas and they created the rubber ridges on the boot that we are still used to today. Since then there have been twelve different variations of the boot, four of which came in the 1990s, and players such as Steven Gerrard, Zinedine Zidane and, of course, David Beckham have worn them throughout their careers. Away from the Preds, Adidas also gave the 1990s Copa Mundials, the French World Cup winning kits of 1998, and provided the footballs for the 1990, 1994 and 1998 World Cup tournaments.

'90s MOMENT

David Beckham made his name on the big stage with his famous goal from the halfway line against Wimbledon in 1996. He was wearing Predator boots.

NIKE

Nike were a bit of a latecomer when it comes to football. It wasn't until the mid-1990s that the American sportswear company really branched out into the sport – but when they did, they did it in style. Fans will fondly remember the adverts of the era that featured Brazilian players showing off their skills around an airport, and the classic good *vs* evil campaign (discussed in more detail later in the book), but it was the 1994 World Cup that saw Nike really enter the 'soccer' market for the first time. The company's Tiempo boot was the first big release, and ten players actually wore it in the tournament's final, including Romario and Paolo Maldini. The competition was the big exposure the company needed and they followed up their World Cup success by signing Eric Cantona and Ian Wright to their roster. By the time the battle against the devil's army came about, Luis Figo, Patrick Kluivert and Edgar Davids were all Nike endorsed too. Then, in 1998, Nike released their first-ever Mercurial boot, worn and launched by Brazilian striker Ronaldo for the World Cup in France. By this point Nike had entered the kit arena as well, supplying Brazil, USA and the Netherlands for the '98 finals, and later entered the domestic market with Arsenal becoming the first English club to wear Nike sportswear. Now one of the game's market leaders, 2013 saw them secure one of football's biggest deals, the England national team kits.

PUMA

Children of the decade will rejoice in union about Puma's biggest input into the era's nostalgia – the Puma King boot. However, the brand's most famous piece of footwear goes way back, further than the era we are celebrating, and were first made for Portuguese legend Eusébio as an homage to him winning the 1966 FIFA Golden Boot. Since that iconic boot, names such as Cruyff and Maradona donned the Kings, and by 1990 it was one of the leaders in boot choices. The decade saw Puma switch up boot design by bringing out Puma Kings in both all white and dark red, and it's those colourings that made it a popular boot of the era. Puma were also consistent kit suppliers during this time, with Leeds, Sheffield Wednesday, and a wrath of international sides across the World Cups of 1994 and 1998, sporting the feline on their chests.

WORTH A MENTION

We've discussed the big hitters of the decade, but they weren't the only option when it came to kickers on a football pitch. Reebok were the chosen supplier of Ryan Giggs and Andy Cole. John Fashanu spent most of his career wearing Quasar boots, along with Gary Lineker, while Matt Le Tissier was often seen in Hi-Tec throughout the decade. Coloured boots were a trend creeping in during this time with Valsport leading the way with various different options away from the traditional black. Other names to grace the pitch also included Arrow, Hummel, Fila, Uhlsport, Diadora, Lotto and Mizuno.

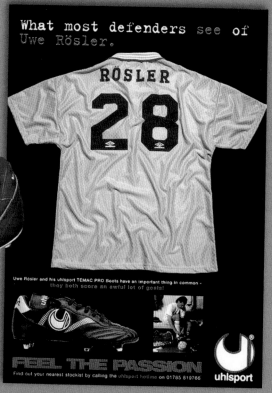

CUP WINNERS' CUP

It used to be so simple, win the FA Cup and the following season you'd be battling it out with cup winners from around Europe for the Cup Winners' Cup. Yet in their infinite wisdom, UEFA decided to merge this competition with the UEFA Cup and create the Europa League. Why? Well, after the Champions League expansion in 1997 that saw more than one team from each country enter, it was said that the level of interest and calibre of teams in the CWC had declined. However, having seen now how clubs treat the Europa League, in hindsight this abolition of the competition could be questioned.

The CWC began in 1960, and three years later Tottenham Hotspur lifted the trophy after a 5–1 win over Atlético Madrid, becoming the first English team to win a European cup. And the 1990s brought about some memorable moments for the competition and for English clubs. Manchester United's 1991 win over Barcelona marked the first season of reintroduction of English clubs to European competition following the Heysel disaster. There were also CWC final wins for Arsenal (1–0 over Parma in 1994) and Chelsea (1–0 over Stuttgart in 1998). A year later Lazio beat Real Mallorca in the competition's final game.

'90s MOMENT

The competition holds good and bad memories for Arsenal. Their 1994 win was followed by a 2–1 defeat to Real Zaragoza the following year, with an extra-time winner from ex-Tottenham star Nayim. His looping volley from fully 40 yards beat David Seaman in the last minute of extra time.

ZENITH DATA SYSTEMS CUP

With English teams banned from Europe in 1985, the decision was made to introduce a new cup competition to go alongside the FA Cup and League Cup. The Full Members Cup was launched and consisted of teams from only the top two divisions, with the inaugural competition being won by Chelsea in a 5–4 victory over Manchester City at Wembley in March 1986. It was later sponsored, firstly by Simod, and then in the 1990s by computer hardware company Zenith Data Systems. There were three finals in the 1990s, with Chelsea beating Middlesbrough, Crystal Palace overcoming Everton, and finally, Nottingham Forest's 1992 win over Southampton. The competition was then cancelled with the launch of the new Premier League, but it remains one of the favourite 'do you remember' cup competitions.

ANGLO-ITALIAN CUP

Following the removal of the Zenith Data Systems Cup, there came a fondly remembered continental competition, the Anglo-Italian Cup. Its roots actually date back to the 1970s, when the competition was first launched and played intermittently until 1986. The 1992 version consisted of just teams from England's newly named First Division and the Serie B in Italy. All twenty-four teams competed in the preliminary rounds, with the main competition coming down to four groups of four from each nation. The top two from each then progressed to a regional semi-final before a trip to Wembley to face the opposing best. The competition lasted four seasons, with wins for Cremonese over Derby, Brescia over Notts County, Notts County over Ascoli in 1995 (the only English win), and finally Genoa 5–2 over Port Vale. The competition was abandoned the following season citing increasing violence and failure to organise fixture dates.

EVENING STANDARD FIVES

These days, five-a-side football is more suited to a kick-around on a weeknight after work, or a way for professionals to end a tough training session. Back in the 1990s, though, clubs used to regularly send their first team players to compete in televised indoor five-a-side competitions – most notably in London, where the Evening Standard Fives was a popular competition full of the decade's most famous names. The capital's finest teams took part and, as hard as it is to imagine Arsène Wenger sending his troops down for a friendly kick-about in 2013, it was a rare treat for spectators in the 1990s. Here we see the victorious Wycombe Wanderers team after their win in 1994, a year before the competition was cancelled.

SQUAD NUMBERS

Fans of football in the 1970s and '80s grew up on numbers 1–11, while modern supporters think nothing of seeing a plethora of different numbers on match day. As 1990s children, we fall somewhere in the middle. Although World Cups had seen squad numbers used for a number of years, 1–11 was still being used until the FA introduced both names and numbers on the back of shirts for the start of the 1993/94 season, with the Football League following suit six years later. The '93-style font may now look like some dodgy knock-off from a market-stall, but it was used until 1997.

'90S MOMENT

We may be used to ridiculously high squad numbers now, but back in 1997 when Inter Milan signed Brazilian superstar Ronaldo, his insistence for the number 9 shirt put then holder Ivan Zamorano's nose right out of joint. So much so, he changed his number to 1+8 instead of 18.

MATCH DAY PROGRAMMES

They are part of the furniture on match day, and you either ignore or collect, but there's something about a programme that is just part of the whole experience. Nothing new to the 1990s, programmes have been going since way back in the 1880s when a single piece of card was used to show the date and teams. The 1990s, however, saw programmes progress into magazines rather than simple guides to the day's game. With interviews, features and opposition focus, the now full-colour publications became the perfect pre-match ritual read. They remain very much part of football culture today, with this writer having a loft full of them.

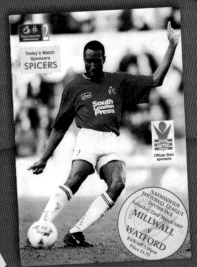

FANZINES

Before the days of fans' forums and messageboards, there were very few ways for fans to get their points across on the state of their favourite football club. The most popular sounding board was the football fanzine – a publication made for the fans, by the fans and normally sold around the ground before games. With football supporters always having plenty to say, there was a boom in fanzines in the late 1980s and early 1990s, with the majority of the league clubs each having their own publication. Since then, sadly, the advent of the internet and in particular blogging has seen a demise in this type of publication, and very few have continued publishing. Currently Bradford City's *The City Gent* is the longest running fanzine, now in its twenty-sixth season. However, it's one of the few remaining exceptions.

THE PREMIER LEAGUE

You could write a whole book on how the Premier League changed football. I'm not here to do that, but any look back at the 1990s can't go by without mentioning the establishment of a league that turned football on its head. First agreed on 17 July 1991, all twenty-two top division teams resigned from the 104-year-old Football League's First Division and on 27 May 1992, the Premier League was born. Over the next eight seasons, backed by Sky and their multi-million pound deal (more on that later), the Carling sponsored league soon brought the game's biggest names to England and paved the way for England's top tier to be one of the best, if not *the* best in football today.

THE CHAMPIONS LEAGUE

It wasn't just England's top flight that got a makeover, the European Cup, the continent's premier competition, was also revamped in 1992, becoming the Champions League. UEFA added a group stage to the previous straight knockout competition and later allowed more than one team from each nation to participate – even if that did make the initial premise of a competition between Europe's champions redundant. The first season of the Champions League in 1992/93 did see only champions and was won by Marseille (although they were later stripped of the title, due to match-fixing). England's only victory in the 1990s came right at the end of the decade when Manchester United sealed an epic treble by beating Bayern Munich at the Nou Camp in 1999's final.

'90s MOMENT

The inaugural season of the Champions League saw a real Battle of Britain in the second round as English champions Leeds United took on Scottish champions Rangers. Over the two legs it was north of the border that celebrated victory with a 4–2 aggregate win.

RULES

The 1990s bought about some big rule changes in football too, easily changing the game both on and off the pitch. The Taylor Report was already in full swing at the top of the decade, and meant that by the middle of the 1990s all-seater stadiums were the norm, as we said farewell to the age of terraces at top-level football grounds. On the pitch, the back-pass rule was implemented in 1992 to speed up the game and stop time wasting by defenders and goalkeepers. It meant that goalies could no longer pick up the ball when intentionally kicked to them by a teammate – needless to say it brought some early nerves to keepers at the start of that campaign.

The biggest change to football, however, came thanks to little known Belgium midfielder Jean-Marc Bosman. In 1995 he took his club RFC Liège to court for preventing his move to Dunkerque at the end of his contract. On 15 December the court ruled in favour of Bosman, citing that the transfer system placed restrictions on the free movement of works. Thus changing the way football deals with transfers in the most dramatic way, and giving more power to the players. From that point on, players were free to leave clubs for nothing at the end of their contracts and were permitted to sign 'pre-contract agreements' six months before expiry. The first such example came when Edgar Davids moved from Ajax to AC Milan in 1996, while Steve McManaman became the first high-profile Brit to take advantage of the rule when he moved from Liverpool to Real Madrid in 1999.

JEAN-MARC BOSMAN
CLUB LIEGEOIS

WHO WON WHAT

Here is a guide to who won what during the 1990s. Manchester United dominated the decade, winning every major trophy bar the UEFA Cup. There was also significant silverware for Arsenal and Liverpool while Barcelona's first-ever European Cup win came at Wembley in 1992.

First Division/Premier League
1990 Liverpool
1991 Arsenal
1992 Leeds United
1993 Manchester United
1994 Manchester United
1995 Blackburn Rovers
1996 Manchester United
1997 Manchester United
1998 Arsenal
1999 Manchester United

Second/First Division
1990 Leeds United
1991 Oldham Athletic
1992 Ipswich Town
1993 Newcastle United
1994 Crystal Palace
1995 Middlesbrough
1996 Sunderland
1997 Bolton Wanderers
1998 Nottingham Forest
1999 Sunderland

Third/Second Division
1990 Bristol Rovers
1991 Cambridge United
1992 Brentford
1993 Stoke City
1994 Reading
1995 Birmingham City
1996 Swindon Town
1997 Bury
1998 Watford
1999 Fulham

Zenith Data Systems Cup
1990 Chelsea
1991 Crystal Palace
1992 Nottingham Forest

Fourth/Third Division

1990 Exeter City
1991 Darlington
1992 Burnley
1993 Cardiff City
1994 Shrewsbury Town
1995 Carlisle United
1996 Preston North End
1997 Wigan Athletic
1998 Notts County
1999 Brentford

FA Cup

1990 Manchester United
1991 Tottenham Hotspur
1992 Liverpool
1993 Arsenal
1994 Manchester United
1995 Everton
1996 Manchester United
1997 Chelsea
1998 Arsenal
1999 Manchester United

League Cup

1990 Nottingham Forest
1991 Sheffield Wednesday
1992 Manchester United
1993 Arsenal
1994 Aston Villa
1995 Liverpool
1996 Aston Villa
1997 Leicester City
1998 Chelsea
1999 Tottenham Hotspur

European Cup/Champions League

1990 AC Milan
1991 Red Star Belgrade
1992 Barcelona
1993 Marseille
1994 AC Milan
1995 Ajax
1996 Juventus
1997 Borussia Dortmund
1998 Real Madrid
1999 Manchester United

UEFA Cup

1990 Juventus
1991 Inter Milan
1992 Ajax
1993 Juventus
1994 Inter Milan
1995 Parma
1996 Bayern Munich
1997 Schalke
1998 Inter Milan
1999 Parma

Cup Winners' Cup

1990 Sampdoria
1991 Manchester United
1992 Werder Bremen
1993 Parma
1994 Arsenal
1995 Real Zaragoza
1996 Paris St Germain
1997 Barcelona
1998 Chelsea
1999 Lazio

2

ITALIA '90

THE TOURNAMENT

The fourteenth World Cup came back to Europe after the sizzlin' summer of the 1986 tournament in Mexico and was hosted by Italy for a second time. The upgrading of twelve stadiums took more time than planned and the organisers feared they would have to start the competition with some of the stadiums unfinished, but everything was perfect by 8 June 1990, the date for the opening match in Milan. And what an opening match it was, with Cameroon beating reigning champions Argentina 1–0. The Lions would then go on to beat Romania in their next game with 38-year-old Roger Milla stealing the show, scoring both goals and giving the world the *Milla wiggle* celebration – c'mon you know you've done it.

With Pavarotti's *Nessun Dorma* ringing in their ears, hosts Italy sailed through their group stage sweeping aside USA, Austria and Czechoslovakia with goals from little-known front man Salvatore 'Totò' Schillaci. West Germany also dominated their group scoring nine goals in their opening two games, while there were impressive early performances from Yugoslavia and Costa Rica. Ireland enjoyed their first ever World Cup, finishing above Netherlands in Group F and then winning a memorable penalty shoot-out over Romania thanks to the heroics of Packie Bonner and David O'Leary's winner. The knockout stage also pitted old enemies West Germany and Netherlands, in a game that's best remembered for a confrontation between Frank Rijkaard and Rudi Völler that ended with the Dutchman spitting into the mullet of the Germany star.

Ultimately it was the World Cup for the old powers, with all the previous winners present, and the final four included big hitters West Germany, England, Italy and Argentina. Two heart-breaking semi-finals later and it was the Germans and Diego Maradona's side that headed to Rome for the 1990 World Cup final. It was a final low on quality, as the two battled through a bruising showpiece that saw Argentine Pedro Monzon become the first player to be sent off in a World Cup final, and Andreas Brehme notch an eighty-fifth minute winner from the penalty spot for West Germany, who'd lift their third World Cup trophy.

It's now regarded as one of the most defensive tournaments, but for anyone who grew up in the 1990s, Italia '90 was very much the catalyst for our future as football fans.

Argentina 0 Cameroon 1
8th June 1990

SIERRA LEONE LE15

THE MASCOT

In the crazy world of football mascots, the 1990 representative was easily the most mind-boggling of any major tournament (London 2012 Olympic's ridiculous attempt included). Ciao was his name and he was well … a stick figure. Decked out in Italy's tricolore and named after the Italian greeting, the football-headed Lego-looking mascot was effortless but very cool – especially when he was seen kicking a ball on the original TV graphics. He had more control than some of the UAE players, that's for sure.

Bobby Robson's England arrived in Italy looking to put the dark days of 1980s football behind them and shine a light back on the national game. What they achieved went beyond all that, finishing fourth place and giving England its finest hour on the world stage since 1966. New Order sang and John Barnes rapped England into the group stage with *World in Motion*, with a team that looked as good as any going into the finals. In Peter Shilton they had one of the best goalkeepers in the world, supporting a defence anchored by Des Walker and Stuart Pearce. Barnes, Gascoigne and Robson provided the creativity, with Mexico 86's Golden Boot winner Gary Lineker in attack.

The group stage started slowly but effectively; draws with Ireland and a talented Holland side preceded a 1–0 win over Egypt that meant that England topped the group. Belgium were next and it took a David Platt volley in the last minute of extra time to see England through to an intriguing and pulsating quarter-final with Cameroon. After Platt's opener, England rallied from 2–1 down to beat the impressive Cameroon with two nerve-biting penalties from Gary Lineker, and another star turn from Gazza. For all its talents, however, Robson's team would be derailed in the semi-finals by familiar foes West Germany. Brehme and Lineker traded goals in normal time, Gascoigne shed his famous tears, but against the backdrop of Turin, Stuart Pearce and a mullet-less Chris Waddle both missed spot-kicks to send the Three Lions home. Their performance may not have won them medals, but back home England fell in love with football again and the disappointment from a nation was summed up by the tears of their new hero wearing number 19.

1	Peter Shilton	GK
2	Gary Stevens	DF
3	Stuart Pearce	DF
4	Neil Webb	MF
5	Des Walker	DF
6	Terry Butcher	DF
7	Bryan Robson (c)	MF
8	Chris Waddle	MF
9	Peter Beardsley	FW
10	Gary Lineker	FW
11	John Barnes	MF
12	Paul Parker	DF
13	Chris Woods	GK
14	Mark Wright	DF
15	Tony Dorigo	DF
16	Steve McMahon	MF
17	David Platt	MF
18	Steve Hodge	MF
19	Paul Gascoigne	MF
20	Trevor Steven	MF
21	Steve Bull	FW
22	Dave Beasant	GK

THE RESULTS

Group A
Austria, **Czechoslovakia**, **Italy**, USA

Italy	1–0	Austria
USA	1–5	Czechoslovakia
Italy	1–0	USA
Czechoslovakia	1–0	Austria
Austria	2–1	USA
Italy	2–0	Czechoslovakia

Group B
Argentina, **Cameroon**, **Romania**, USSR

Argentina	0–1	Cameroon
USSR	0–2	Romania
Argentina	2–0	USSR
Cameroon	2–1	Romania
Argentina	1–1	Romania
Cameroon	0–4	USSR

Group C
Brazil, **Costa Rica**, Scotland, Sweden

Brazil	2–1	Sweden
Costa Rica	1–0	Scotland
Brazil	1–0	Costa Rica
Sweden	1–2	Scotland
Brazil	1–0	Scotland
Sweden	1–2	Costa Rica

Group D
Colombia, UAE, **West Germany**, **Yugoslavia**

UAE	0–2	Colombia
West Germany	4–1	Yugoslavia
Yugoslavia	1–0	Colombia
West Germany	5–1	UAE
West Germany	1–1	Colombia
Yugoslavia	4–1	UAE

Group E
Belgium, South Korea, **Spain**, Uruguay

Belgium	2–0	South Korea
Uruguay	0–0	Spain
Belgium	3–1	Uruguay
South Korea	1–3	Spain
Belgium	1–2	Spain
South Korea	0–1	Uruguay

Group F
England, Egypt, Ireland, **Netherlands**

England	1–1	Ireland
Netherlands	1–1	Egypt
England	0–0	Netherlands
Ireland	0–0	Egypt
England	1–0	Egypt
Ireland	1–1	Netherlands

Second Round

West Germany	2–1	Netherlands
Czechoslovakia	4–1	Costa Rica
England	1–0	Belgium (aet)
Cameroon	2–1	Colombia (aet)
Italy	2–0	Uruguay
Ireland	0–0	Romania (Ireland won 5–4 on pens)
Spain	1–2	Yugoslavia (aet)
Brazil	0–1	Argentina

Quarter-finals

West Germany	1–0	Czechoslovakia
England	3–2	Cameroon (aet)
Italy	1–0	Ireland
Yugoslavia	0–0	Argentina (Argentina won 3–2 on pens)

Semi-finals
West Germany 1–1 England
(West Germany won 4–3 on pens)

Italy 1–1 Argentina
(Argentina won 4–3 on pens)

Third place play-off
Italy 2–1 England

Final
West Germany 1–0 Argentina

'90s MOMENT

The 1990s would witness many ups and downs for Paul Gascoigne, but the season following Italia '90 will be remembered for Spurs' Gazza-inspired run to the FA Cup final, including the memorable semi-final free kick against Arsenal.

THE STARS

TOTÒ SCHILLACI

Major tournaments have a history of unlikely heroes, and at Italia '90 Totò Schillaci became the yardstick to what all-future breakout stars are referred to. The little Juventus striker actually made his debut during the finals as a sub in the Italian's first game, netting the winner against Austria. He went on to score six goals and win the tournament's Golden Boot, becoming a household name in the process.

LOTHAR MATTHÄUS

The powerhouse in midfield that epitomised the West Germany team of 1990, Italia '90 was the perfect tournament for the Inter Milan man. Having represented his country at both the 1982 and 1986 tournaments, Matthäus led by example in Italy, scoring four goals and captaining his nation to their third World Cup win. He would later go on to break the record for most World Cup games for a single outfield player.

3

THE MUSIC

WORLD IN MOTION

Football songs went down a different path in the 1990s, most were cooler, more serious and, without discarding the *Back Homes* and *Anfield Raps* of the 1970s and '80s, actual pop songs. There were none cooler, though, than the song that kicked off the decade and became the backdrop to Italia '90 – *World In Motion*. Simply put, *World In Motion* changed football songs. It didn't just roll out the England squad and give them a cheesy ditty to sing, it was New Order – a proper, well-known band – and a song that became a number one hit. Written by comedian Keith Allen, New Order members Steve Morris and Gillian Gilbert then used a theme already written for BBC's youth current affairs show *Reportage* to create the music for

the track. Mischievously Allen attempted to sneak a drug reference into the song by calling it *E for England* but it was quickly vetoed by the FA before the song's release on 21 May 1990.

Although New Order performed the single, the England team were also involved and sung along to the chorus and appeared in the video. The icing on the cake for the track, though, came with John Barnes' brilliant rap in the second half of the song. Selected to perform it ahead of Peter Beardsley, Paul Gascoigne and Chris Waddle, Barnes breezed through the lyrics like a young Run-D.M.C. and got everyone quickly singing along to his 'master plan' and being an 'England man'. Just like most children in the 1990s should know the lyrics to the *Fresh Prince of Bel-Air* theme, football fans of the same era should be able to match Barnsey's words beat for beat too. It hit number one in the UK singles chart in June 1990 and stayed there for two weeks, before Elton John's *Sacrifice* knocked it off top spot. It remains New Order's only ever chart-topper.

FOG ON THE TYNE

The 1990 World Cup made Paul Gascoigne a bona fide superstar. He returned home a hero and it wasn't long before you couldn't turn on the TV or pick up a magazine without seeing the Geordie maestro's beaming face. So what is a superstar to do with his newfound fame? Release a pop record of course! Returning to his roots, he teamed up with hometown band Lindisfarne for a reworked version of a track from their 1971 album called *Fog On The Tyne*. Having obviously picked up tips from John Barnes, Gazza waxed lyrical on the track about his rise to fame, lads from the Toon and his love for sausage rolls. Highlights from the video included him sailing down the Tyne wearing his trademark Gazza shellsuit, and dance moves that were a sure sign of Tyneside on a Saturday night. The England star's popularity meant the song reached number two in the charts and gave Lindisfarne a rare moment of mainstream music fame.

COME ON YOU REDS

FA Cup final songs were born in the 1970s, but none have been more successful than Manchester United's 1994 showpiece track *Come On You Reds*. Released four weeks prior to the 1994 final that saw the Red Devils take on Glen Hoddle's Chelsea, the song included Status Quo and an adaptation of their song *Burning Bridges*. Changing the lyrics to suit United, the song included a rundown of the squad (even managing to get the name Kanchelskis into a lyric) and the famous *Glory, Glory, Man Utd* terrace chant. It spent fifteen weeks in the UK singles chart, becoming the only club song to ever reach number one in May of that year, before being dislodged by Wet, Wet, Wet's juggernaut *Love Is All Around*.

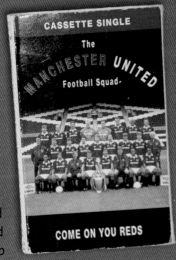

The 1990s also saw three more United songs enter the charts; the 1995 follow up *We're Gonna Do It Again* (which is less remembered because, well, they didn't), and then a year later the dance-fuelled *Move, Move, Move (The Red Tribe)* which reached number six and included a video of some of the elder United players struggling to keep up with the high-octane number. Lastly, United ended the decade by missing out on the top ten with *Lift It High (All About Belief)* which sounded like a more credible serious music route, but most Old Trafford fans would probably struggle to remember the 1999 indie-inspired effort.

'90s MOMENT

Manchester United recorded their first ever League and Cup double in 1994, regaining their Premier League crown ahead of Blackburn Rovers, before beating Chelsea 4–0 in the FA Cup final at Wembley.

DO THE RIGHT THING

Songs by football clubs are one thing, songs for national tournaments quite an acceptable other, but serious solo efforts by footballers? Well, that's something that has never gone down too well. Ever since Waddle and Hoddle performed contrasting performances on *Top of the Pops* during the previous decade, footballers have been ill-advised to take themselves too seriously when it comes to music.

Gazza had shown already that it's better to make a novelty record, but somehow Ian Wright failed to take notice. So, in 1993, the Arsenal star teamed up with Pet Shop Boys' Chris Lowe to write and release *Do The Right Thing*. The message was admirable, as Wright had a somewhat controversial reputation at the time, but unfortunately the delivery wasn't. It only reached number forty-three in the UK singles chart and is better remembered for the video, in which Wright is seen wearing a questionable hat and dancing around what can only be described as 1990s disco meets indoor five-a-side pitch – maybe not the right call on that one, Ian!

PASS & MOVE
(IT'S THE LIVERPOOL GROOVE)

The 1996 FA Cup final saw England's two biggest clubs clash at Wembley, as Manchester United took on old rivals Liverpool. The match never actually lived up to the billing and it needed an Eric Cantona winner to lift a dire final. But, whereas Liverpool may have lost the battle on the pitch, they won the war in the charts against United. *United's Move, Move, Move (The Red Tribe)* reached number six in May 1996 but was usurped by Liverpool's own Cup final song, *Pass & Move (It's the Liverpool Groove)* which reached number four. The track that also featured the Boot Room Boyz, included another rap for MC John Barnes and an over-repeated bridge ode to Robbie Fowler that consisted of the players singing, 'Go Robbie, go Robbie go!' No wonder it never quite hit the highs of the *Anfield Rap*.

'90s MOMENT

Easily the fashion faux pas of the 1990s, Liverpool decided on cream Armani suits for the pre-match walk around the pitch. A decision made by goalkeeper David James, it led to the Anfield squad being labelled the 'Spice Boys'.

3 LIONS

'It's coming home' – three simple words, but three simple words that would be the theme song for the summer of 1996. It created a new legacy among football fans and is often regarded as the most popular football anthem of all time.

With Britpop dominating the UK charts in the mid-1990s, the FA asked Lightning Seeds' (whose own tune *Life of Riley* was regularly being used as the theme for *Match of the Day*'s Goal of the Month) Ian Broudie to record a song for Euro 96, which was to be hosted by England. Broudie was apprehensive at first, telling the *1000 UK Number One Hits*, 'I would never have bought a football single myself and I certainly didn't want to do one of those cheerleading records. Being a fan is about losing and, if we did it, I wanted to write it from a fan's point of view.'

So enter comedians David Baddiel and Frank Skinner; red hot from their popular TV show *Fantasy Football League*, Broudie enlisted their help to write a new England song that played on England's misfortunes at previous tournaments. That song was *3 Lions*. Released on 1 June 1996, it rocketed to the top of the charts, thanks to the catchy lyrics that also incorporated some of England's most memorable moments, including Bobby Moore's tackle in 1970 and Nobby Stiles' celebratory dance of 1966. It captured both the mood of the nation and the England football team as Terry Venables' men progressed to the semi-finals, and stadiums around the country echoed to the sound of fans singing their new England anthem. It was so popular in fact, that even the other nations embraced it, and the song even charted in Germany at number sixteen thanks to the players singing it during their victory parade. It was a UK number one twice during that summer, and eventually stayed in the charts for fifteen weeks.

'The song has passed into folklore. Every time there's a big match, you can guarantee that some newspaper will be quoting from the song in their headlines.' Broudie's not wrong.

Two years later, after England had suffered more penalty heartbreak at Euro '96, the boys decided to re-record the song and released *3 Lions '98* as an unofficial anthem. Updating the lyrics to include more modern references like Paul Ince's bloody image after a qualifier against Italy and Stuart Pearce's Spain celebration of two years before, the track once again debuted at number one and stayed top of the pile for three weeks, far outselling the FA's official England song.

The video is also often fondly remembered for Frank Skinner's do-it-yourself World Cup trophy, dipping his hand in custard while holding a melon to portray the famous gold globe. There was also a nod to German Euro '96 star Stefan Kuntz, with German players wearing the name 'Kuntz' on the back of their shirts. Well, if you're going to make a point …

ENGLAND'S IRIE

3 Lions wasn't the only football song in 1996 – Keith Allen was back and this time brought along Shaun Ryder's Black Grape for *England's Irie*. The upbeat anthem also featured Joe Strummer (formerly of The Clash) and reached number six at the end of June 1996. Possibly more underrated than many other England songs, the lyrics did have the perfect mix of Allen-inspired comedy and lines easily chanted in a football stadium but was just overshadowed by Skinner, Baddiel and their theme tune of the summer. 'Cut the trigger, I fire like this!'

'90s MOMENT

One of Sky Sports' Martin Tyler's most famous lines of commentary came as Arsenal clinched their first Premier League title in 1998. As Tony Adams fired in the Gunners' third goal against Everton Tyler screamed, 'Would you believe it!', which has now been used on countless Sky adverts.

Having seen the likes of New Order, The Lightning Seeds and even Status Quo get involved with football songs in the 1990s, long-time Chelsea fan Suggs seized his opportunity when the Blues reached the FA Cup final of 1997. Adding a catchy Madness-esque twang to the football market, *Blue Day* hit the charts in May 1997 and reached a high of twenty-two in the UK Top 40.

HOT STUFF

As much as football songs became more credible during the 1990s, there were a few that still reeked of the smelliest stilton and this Arsenal song from 1998 was definitely one of them. And how we loved it! Playing on the fact that the Gunners had gone from the 'boring, boring' days under George Graham to Arsène Wenger's free-flowing future of football, they released a reworked version of Donna Summer's 'Hot Stuff' in May 1998. Using samples from the original, and replacing lyrics to suit the club and current players, it peeked at number nine in the UK Top 40 in a season that also saw Arsenal

Arsenal F.C.

'90s MOMENT

Chelsea made it a Blue Day in 1997 thanks to the then fastest goal in FA Cup final history from Roberto Di Matteo. The Italian scored after just twenty-seven seconds, as the Blues beat Middlesbrough 2–0 at Wembley.

(HOW DOES IT FEEL TO BE) ON TOP OF THE WORLD?

Having dabbled with credible artists for both 1990 and 1996 official England songs, the FA went one better in 1998 and gathered a whole line-up of popular acts to form 'England United'. Combining indie bands Echo & The Bunnymen and Ocean Colour Scene with the Spice Girls, England United's *(How Does It Feel to Be) On Top of the World* went back to a celebratory tone after *3 Lions*, but the reaction was lukewarm from England fans.

It debuted at number nine in the official charts but crashed out of the top ten a week later, and was left trailing by both *3 Lions '98* and *Vindaloo*. There was a more laid-back approach to the video too; players only made small appearances while the bands simply had a kick-about in a make-believe backyard as they morphed from kids to adults. Doesn't actually sound so laid back when you put it like that, though.

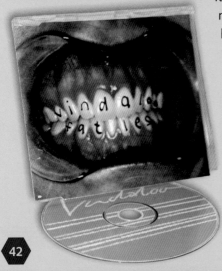

VINDALOO

After his success of *World in Motion* and input on *England's Irie*, Keith Allen returned to the football song arena in 1998 with comedy inspired *Vindaloo* under the name Fat Les. Made up of Allen, Blur bassist Alex James and artist Damien Hirst, Fat Les' *Vindaloo* was meant as a parody to traditional England songs, but was quickly adopted by fans due to its catchy 'nah nah nah' hook and chant-like lyrics such as 'We're gonna score one more than you'. It reached number two in the UK charts on 20 June 1998 and stayed there for three weeks, with only *3 Lions* preventing it from hitting top spot.

Vindaloo's video was an equally well-received success; using The Verve's *Bittersweet Symphony* as its model, it had a Richard Ashcroft look-a-like walking through the same streets to the tune of *Vindaloo*. In Fat Les' version, however, he was not alone and was joined by some famous faces, including Matt Lucas, David Walliams and a young Lily Allen, as well as a priest, some sumo wrestlers and scantily-clad maids and nurses – all holding bags of their favourite Indian cuisine, of course.

EAT MY GOAL

Collapsed Lung are a name you're probably not too familiar with, but you'll know their most famous song, *Eat My Goal*, which was released along with a wave of football songs around the 1998 World Cup. Although it never hit the Top 10 (eighteen was its highest position), it has since been used on countless adverts and VTs, most notably for Coca-Cola.

OUTSTANDING

Gazza kicked off the decade with his solo record and the 1990s ended with yet another footballer crossing the musical line, Andrew Cole. Back then he was still just Andy, and his track was *Outstanding* (that's the name of it, not a description), released in September 1999. Clearly learning nothing from Ian Wright years before him, Cole bobbed along to the track in his flash sports car and rapped his way through, citing he was 'sharp like a razor' with 'speed to amaze ya' among other things. Sadly for the treble-winning Manchester United star, his track never lit up the pop charts, only reaching number sixty-eight.

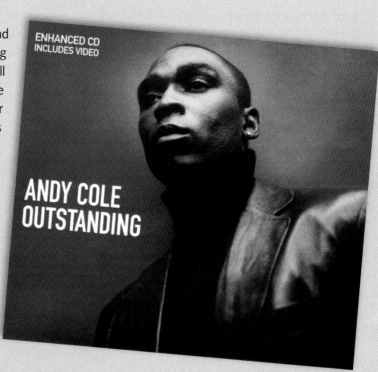

ENHANCED CD
INCLUDES VIDEO

ANDY COLE
OUTSTANDING

'90s MOMENT

Andy Cole became the first player to score five goals in a Premier League match when he notched his famous five in Manchester United's 9–0 mauling of Ipswich in March 1995.

THE BEAUTIFUL GAME

Euro '96 gave music the chance to cash in on an entirely football orientated album, using all the songs fans had now associated with the beautiful game – hence the name of the album. The Britpop inspired LP featured songs from Blur, Supergrass, Lightning Seeds and Pulp, as well as the summer's footballing theme tune *3 Lions*. It even had some comical sketches from Baddiel and Skinner, discussing the lyrics to their anthem and wondering if The Wannadies was an anagram of Dennis Wise.

WORTH A MENTION

Outside of Italia '90 and Pavarotti's *Nessun Dorma*, official tournament songs were worth avoiding during the 1990s. Simply Red's *We're in This Together* for Euro '96 and France '98's *Cup of Life* by Ricky Martin were two that are easily forgotten. However, 1998 did see a decent effort from Chumbawumba and *Top of The World (Olé, Olé, Olé)*, along with Dario G's dance track *Carnival de Paris*. Elsewhere, Scotland provided their own tournament songs with Rod Stewart's *Purple Heather* in 1996 and *Don't Come Home Too Soon* by Del Amitri for the World Cup two years later. On the club front, Chelsea preceded *Blue Day* with 1994's Cup final song *No One Can Stop Us Now* while Middlesbrough celebrated 1997's final by releasing *Let's Dance* with comedian Bob Mortimer.

4

EURO '92

THE TOURNAMENT

The European Championships of 1992 took place against a backdrop of political change throughout Europe. The biggest beneficiaries of the changes were Denmark who were called in as last-minute replacements for Yugoslavia due to the outbreak of civil war in the country. The Danes, who had finished a point behind Yugoslavia, were given just two weeks to prepare for the tournament, but it proved to be a memorable finals. The USSR had already qualified ahead of Italy but the country was broken up before the tournament began and they therefore competed under the auspices of the Commonwealth of Independent States (CIS), representing Russia, Ukraine, Belarus, Kazakhstan, Uzbekistan, Turkmenistan, Kyrgyzstan, Armenia, Azerbaijan, Moldova and Tajikistan. Also, for the first time Germany competed as one nation, following the reunification of the East and West in 1990.

When the action did get underway, the eight qualified teams split into two groups with the top two from each progressing to the semi-finals.

WEMBLEY

STOCKHOLM • NORRKOPING • GOTHENBURG • MALMO

EUROPEAN CHAMPIONSHIP 1992

Group A   Group B

Semi-Finals

V

V

Final

V

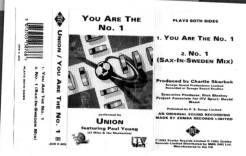

You Are The No. 1

PLAYS BOTH SIDES

1. You Are The No. 1
2. No. 1 (Sax-In-Sweden Mix)

Produced by Charlie Skarbek
Savage Sound Productions Limited
Recorded at Savage Sound Studios

Executive Producer: Rick Blaskey
Project Associate for ITV Sport: David Wood

Published by P. S. Songs Limited

AN ORIGINAL SOUND RECORDING
MADE BY ZOMBA RECORDS LIMITED

performed by

UNION

featuring Paul Young
(of Mike & the Mechanics)

©1992 Zomba Records Limited © 1992 Zomba
Records Limited Distributed by BMG (UK) Ltd.
Manufactured in the UK

Group 1 pitted Sweden with England, France and Denmark. The Swedes proved to be worthwhile hosts, progressing from the group alongside Denmark while England and France were both eliminated without a whimper. Reigning champions Netherlands and World Cup winners Germany qualified from the other group, but they didn't have it all their own way and only Scotland's thumping of CIS in the final game saw both nations progress.

At that stage it seemed a Netherlands v Germany final was on the cards, but Denmark had other ideas. Twice they took the lead in the semi-final against the Dutch, only to be pegged back. Cue Peter Schmeichel to be the hero in the tournament's only penalty shoot-out, saving from Marco van Basten to see Denmark through to the final. Over in Solna, Germany proved too strong for the hosts, Karl-Heinz Riedle's brace seeing them defeat Sweden 3–2.

The final in Gothenburg then saw a heavily fancied Germany side against a team who were both understudies and underdogs for the trophy. Denmark had once again not read the script, however, and thanks to goals from John Jensen and Kim Vilfort they produced one of the greatest ever shocks in international football.

THE MASCOT

Having seen the effort Italy put in for Italia '90, the pressure was on for Sweden to provide something just as imaginative, just as original for Euro '92, and pull a rabbit out of a hat. They did just that, he was a rabbit called, erm, Rabbit, just like the rabbit from Euro '88 only decked out in yellow and blue. Not the most imaginative idea of the 1990s that one.

ENGLAND

The nicest way to describe England and their performances at Euro '92 would be as transitional. Graham Taylor had replaced Bobby Robson after Italia '90 and had the difficult job of following the exploits of the England team in Italy two years previously.
1990 had been the last tournament for many of those players, and only nine of that squad made the final twenty for Sweden. They did include Des Walker, David Platt and Gary Lineker, who was looking for one goal to match Bobby Charlton's goal-scoring record, and with a much simpler route to the finals due to the tournament only having eight teams, fans were optimistic.

Drawn in a group with hosts Sweden, late arrivals Denmark and France, England kicked off the tournament with a goalless draw with the Danes. Another 0–0 against France three days later, however, meant the pressure was on in their last game against the Swedes. They got off to the perfect start when David Platt netted inside the first four minutes, but Sweden took control in the second half, equalising through Jan Eriksson, before Martin Dahlin and Tomas Brolin combined for a delightful winner. Chasing the game, Taylor made the bizarre decision to take off Gary Lineker and replace him with Alan Smith, thus ending Lineker's international career as he was was retiring at the end of the tournament. The plan backfired, England lost and Lineker looked on glumly from the bench. After the game Taylor said, 'We could have done without half time coming, but of course you've got to have half time.' What an insight.

1	Chris Woods	GK
2	Keith Curle	DF
3	Stuart Pearce	DF
4	Martin Keown	DF
5	Des Walker	DF
6	Mark Wright	DF
7	David Platt	MF
8	Trevor Steven	MF
9	Nigel Clough	FW
10	Gary Lineker (c)	FW
11	Andy Sinton	MF
12	Carlton Palmer	MF
13	Nigel Martyn	GK
14	Tony Dorigo	DF
15	Neil Webb	MF
16	Paul Merson	MF
17	Alan Smith	FW
18	Tony Daley	MF
19	David Batty	MF
20	Alan Shearer	FW

THE RESULTS

Group 1
Denmark, England, France, **Sweden**

Sweden	1–1	France
Denmark	0–0	England
France	0–0	England
Sweden	1-0	Denmark
Sweden	2–1	England
France	1–2	Denmark

Group 2
CIS, **Germany**, **Netherlands**, Scotland

Netherlands	1–0	Scotland
CIS	1–1	Germany
Netherlands	0–0	CIS
Scotland	0–2	Germany
Netherlands	3–1	Germany
Scotland	3–0	CIS

Semi-finals
Sweden 2–3 Germany

Netherlands 2–2 Denmark (Denmark won 5–4 on pens)

Final
Germany 0–2 Denmark

THE STARS

TOMAS BROLIN

Brolin hit the headlines during Euro '92 as the home-nation hero who knocked out England. He scored three goals during the tournament, including the wonderfully crafted winner over the Three Lions, and finished joint top scorer along with Henrik Larsson, Dennis Bergkamp and Karl-Heinz Riedle. Somehow the striker was left out of the UEFA team of the tournament, but there was no doubt that he was Euro '92's standout star. It was such a shame that his subsequent move to England with Leeds, and later Crystal Palace, are less remembered for his goals and more for his waistline.

TOMAS BROLIN

JOHN JENSEN

JOHN JENSEN

Peter Schmeichel and Brian Laudrup may have got most of the plaudits, but the alluring image of the Euro '92's final is John Jensen scoring Denmark's opener. The midfielder played in every game for the victorious Danes, and his performances and THAT goal earned him a post-tournament move to the Premier League with Arsenal, where he became a cult hero.

5

TOYS AND GAMES

SUBBUTEO

If you've picked up this book, there should be no need to explain the rules of football's most famous game, Subbuteo. It was about as close to real football as you could possibly get without going outside: eleven players on bases that you finger flick into position around the pitch. No it wasn't easy, so much so that there is now an official tournament for the game, but we all had the game and at least gave it a go at some point in our childhoods.

You can trace the origins of Subbuteo all the way back to 1947, when Peter Adolph invented, manufactured and sold the game by mail order from his home in Tunbridge Wells, Kent. Peter had wanted to call the game 'The Hobby', but the trademark office thought this was too generic so instead he used the Latin name of a bird of prey that was also called hobby, Falco Subbuteo, and the game was born. Over the next thirty years, Peter built the brand and it became a well-known part of football culture, especially in the 1970s when it was at its most popular. It was a game passed down through generations and explains why in the 1990s children were still playing it and why it has a place in this decade too.

By 1990 the classic finger-flicker had gone through a number of changes. After the recession in the 1980s Adolph and his limited company were forced to sell the rights to toy company Waddingtons to keep the game going. Waddingtons updated the range, including more polished grandstands that fitted together better, and produced the first ever floodlights for the game. They also licensed sets for the first time, producing accessories that branded to real life events like Italia '90 and USA '94. The first Premier League ranges also arrived, with all twenty teams having their own boxed set of players. American giants Hasbro acquired Waddingtons in the mid-1990s and again changed the look of the brand, while also removing most of the accessories and streamlining the number of teams available from around 150 to 50, and later only top-flight sides and national teams. The Hasbro sets were, probably, the ones most fondly remembered by kids growing up in the 1990s. They had the giant cloth pitch (that once folded was almost impossible to get the creases out of), the brilliant electronic scoreboard and the spin-off card game Subbuteo Squads.

By the end of the decade the rise in video games meant interest in the game had slowly dwindled, and Hasbro came close to axing the line altogether. However, it remained in special edition sets, and their own computer games until Hasbro relaunched the brand in 2012.

'90s MOMENT

Arsenal's Lee Dixon (seen here playing a spot of Subbuteo with soon never to be seen again Sonny Pike) scored one of the most memorable own goals of all time during the '90s. Playing a simple pass-back to David Seaman, the ball was hit with a bit too much pace and it sailed over Seaman's head and gave Coventry the lead.

TOMY SUPER CUP FOOTBALL

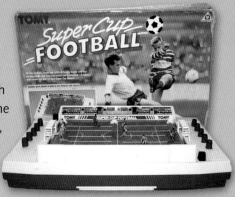

For those who didn't have the patience for the finger flicking of Subbuteo (and I was one of them – much preferring to pick up the players and hit the ball with them), Tomy's Super Cup Football was a fun alternative. First introduced to the market in 1984, Tomy continued to sell this popular product well into the 1990s, despite it making a noise like a broken vacuum cleaner. It features two teams of tiny players who are moved up and down using levers, striking the ball with a platform attached to the boots. The players stay where they are, possibly in homage to some of the rigid tactics of the day, but this meant that sometimes the over-sized ball went into no-man's land where none of the figures could reach it. As it was battery-powered it did make quite a racket, and you were often left with ringing in your ears after a good couple of games. But even the naked-looking spares couldn't prevent this game from being one of the best ever alternatives to Subbuteo.

TOP TRUMPS

The beautiful game has always been about one team being better than the other, and never more so than when playing card game Top Trumps. A playground fave of the 1970s and '80s, it featured boys' themes such as military hardware, modes of transport and racing cars. In the early 1990s, Waddingtons expanded the range to include football in various different guises, including European Club Football teams and Today's Strikers. The aim of the game? To simply better your opponent's score in a choice of different categories. So, if the club on your card has won a high number of league championships you'd pick that figure and challenge your opponent in the same category. Whoever won kept both cards and the game continued until one of the players ran out of Top Trumps cards. Still available today, these cards have kept many of us quiet during long car journeys and rainy days at home.

SPORTSTARS

What young lad doesn't like action figures? Well, it was toy companies Kenner and Tonka who brought about that monumental moment in the 1990s when action figures and football combined to produce Sportstars. These officially licensed products were the first real range of football figures that featured the game's biggest stars. Players from Arsenal, Liverpool, Manchester United, Aston Villa, Everton, Nottingham Forest and Tottenham were covered along with England, Scotland and Wales. Some you'd have to say did not have the best likeness of the player you'd gone out to buy – just try and work out who David Platt and Tony Cottee are among this lot – but they did all come in their own unique poses, with the goalies in full-on 'one for the camera' dive mode.

TERRY VENABLES THE MANAGER

A football game for the purists, Terry Venables The Manager was a proper family board game. A mix of Monopoly, Socceramma and a simple football quiz, the aim of The Manager was to end the game with as much money as possible. Each player chose one or more of eight teams (Man Utd, Man City, Liverpool, Everton, Chelsea, Arsenal, Tottenham or Newcastle) and progressed around the board answering questions on sport, entertainment or general knowledge, to win matches and bag the league championship. It may not be enough, though, as this game was all about collecting the most cash.

FOOTBALL LEAGUE SOCCER QUIZ GAME

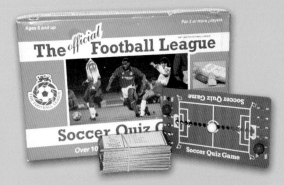

One for the footy stattos this one, the Official Football League Soccer Quiz Game was all about knowing your stuff. The game came with a red ball, a blue ball and a standard white ball, two decks of quiz cards and a green plastic pitch which had a line of holes leading to both goals. The objective was to place the ball in the centre circle, then for every question you got right move one-step closer to goal, the first to score five winning the game. There were various quiz categories to choose from, some much harder than others. I used to particularly excel in the kit questions, but that's maybe because after a good few goes I knew most of the answers by heart anyway.

CORINTHIAN

No toy dominated the latter part of the 1990s more than football figures Corinthians. An idea that started in a pub came to fruition in August 1995 with the launch of the first ever series. At 2.5in high and heads bigger than their bodies, the cartoony but very lifelike figurines debuted with sixteen players from Terry Venables' England squad. I remember first coming across them as a free gift in *Soccer Stars* magazine, and I quickly set about adding to my Paul Ince figure by collecting them all. Along with Ince, the first-ever series was called Headliners and included: David Platt, Andy Cole, Peter Beardsley, Alan Shearer, Ian Wright, Teddy Sheringham, Matthew Le Tissier, Gary Pallister, Tony Adams, Les Ferdinand, David Seaman, Nick Barmby, Darren Anderton, Warren Barton and Stuart Pearce.

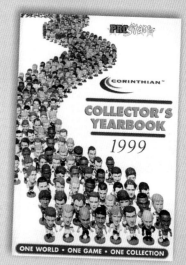

A second series quickly followed to include the first manager in gaffer Venables and secondary squad members such as Steve Howey and Tim Sherwood.

The success on the international front saw Corinthians enter the domestic market at the start of 1996 with a selection of figures for every Premier League club. Some of these first moulds of players were never used again and are now seen as quite rare and valuable. It also remains the only time Corinthians ever released any players for QPR. Updates were continually released for teams throughout the late 1990s, including a new England set for the 1998 World Cup and more international stars to mark this tournament. It was around this time that special edition and bigger versions of the figures were also released. By 1999, the figures now came under the guise 'ProStars'

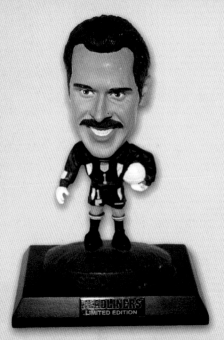

and a set of different domestic and international players came into the shops every six months or so. As a member of their fan club, I still remember excitedly getting their new catalogues and seeing which new faces were being made next – Titi Camara, a memorable favourite. The figures' popularity continued well into the Noughties, adding the 'MircoStars' range to the brand and releasing some fondly collected retro ranges. The company folded in 2009, but the moulds reappeared last year under a new *Soccer Stars* figure line.

SMUGS

What better way to toast your favourite team than by drinking out of a mug bearing one of their famous faces. These bizarre bits of 1990s fun featured mugs, not just decorated with some of the decade's best performers, but with their mush taking over the whole front of the cup. The big plastic faces included Steve McManaman, Alan Shearer, Les Ferdinand, David Seaman, Paul Gascoigne and David Beckham and remains a one-time only series. Not sure why, but I actually still drink out of my Ferdinand one.

SOCCER SUPER HEROES

Bigger was better for this set of figures that hit shops in 1997. Standing 10in high and in full-action poses, this set featured the biggest stars from Arsenal, Manchester United, Liverpool, Tottenham, Newcastle and a Paul Gascoigne Rangers figure. Particular highlights of the range were the inclusion of Robbie Fowler's famous nose clip, Peter Schmeichel's purple and black number and a rare happy looking Roy Keane. The figures didn't stick around for long, though, and this series remained the only release of the range.

CEREAL TOYS

There's nothing quite like the feeling of opening a new box of cereal and rummaging your way through to find a free toy. It's something that is no longer allowed in modern day breakfast treats, but for us in the 1990s it was an added bonus to the morning's routine. In 1995, Sugar Puffs made it even better for us footy fans with a collector series called Honey Monster's Supreme Team. Not the most detailed of football figures, but still worth delving into a box for, the series included Lee Sharpe, Alan Shearer, Ruud Gullit, Les Ferdinand and Ally McCoist. Sugar Puffs also gave away Soccer Toppers in this era – the perfect little accessory to stick on top of your pencils. Featuring many of the sides from the top flight, the mini-kits had squad names and numbers and came in both home and away colours.

Another cereal classic came a year later, when Kellogg's gave the world the Virtual Video Collection to celebrate Euro '96. These were motion-activated holograms that showed clips of current England and Scotland stars in action. When you moved the mini blue screen, the action moved on and showed a goal or save from a recent international – all very hi-tech for 1996. There were sixteen different clips to collect and you could even send off for a special collector's box to keep them in if you wanted to, which looking back now was rather swanky.

'90s MOMENTS

Robbie Fowler scored the fastest ever Premier League hat-trick in 1993, needing just four minutes to net his treble in a 3–1 win over Arsenal at Anfield. On the other side of the spectrum, his 'snorting' celebration against Everton in April 1999 wasn't one of his finest moments.

JIBBA JABBER

The 1990s saw us amused with some strange fads; wrist snappers, colour-changing cars, dancing flowers just to name a few. But perhaps most strange were Jibba Jabbers – a doll that when you shook it, did exactly that, jibbered and jabbered by making the most peculiar sounds. Of course if something is popular, you can guarantee a football spin-off to appear sooner rather than later. So here in all its glory is the football Jibba Jabber, a pencil necked doll with a Robbie Savage hairstyle that made silly sounds.

ALAN SHEARER'S SHOOT-OUT!

Alan Shearer was so good during the 1990s that he could have probably taken on even the best of defences single-handedly. In his own branded board game of the same era, he did exactly that! Alan Shearer's Shoot-Out! was a slightly different take on classic Subbuteo in which there was just a figure of Big Al, up against a set of Brazilian defenders. The idea? Why to score as many goals as possible of course. A clever and addictive game, it's a surprise the concept has never actually been repeated.

WORTH A MENTION

Clever footballing gizmo Kickmaster gave us all the chance to improve our football skills. The toy consisted of a football in a string-like bag with a handle. The aim was to whack the ball as hard as you could without it going anywhere. It also meant you could improve on your ball control. For those of us that like to get messy, Super Cast Soccer was the way to go. One plaster cast and paint job later and you had a magnet or ornament that kind of resembled a football player. Lastly, who could forget those electronic games that kept us busy on the move, despite the stick-figure-like graphics that hardly moved.

6

KITS

For fans of football fashion, the 1990s were easily the high for kit designs. It was anything goes for kit suppliers, as the decade produced some of the best, worst and downright craziest designs ever seen on a football pitch. The shorts went from as close to hot pants as you could get at the beginning of the 1990s, right back to a 1950s long john approach as the decade wore on. Here's my pick of the bunch, which could have covered half the book, with pictures supplied by the excellent www.classicfootballshirts.co.uk.

ARSENAL AWAY 1991/92

Often described as 'the vomit kit' or the bruised banana, either way Arsenal's away kit of 1991 certainly kicked off the decade, well, if not in style, with a sign of what was to come, anyway. Mixing a yellow base with black zigzags that broke up into Adidas lines in between, there was a hell of a lot going on in this jersey that actually lasted for two whole seasons.   Worn by: Andres Limpar, Kevin Campbell

MANCHESTER UNITED AWAY 1991/92

United were kings of the kit design in the 1990s with memorable designs such as the royal blue United badge of 1992 and the Newton Heath coloured halves. However, this 1992 change style ranks number one for me. A paler, more purple-like shade of blue, it was made up of loads of jagged shapes, kind of like the top of a maple leaf.
Worn by: Lee Sharpe, Mike Phelan

NORWICH HOME 1992/94

Norwich fans will always hold this shirt in high regard, as it was worn during the heady days of top five Premier League finishes and European nights, but in reality it's a shocking piece of clothing. Obviously the yellow is hard to ignore with Norwich, so I can forgive makers Ribero for that, but what's with the green and white flakes? It's like one of your Grandma's worst table cloths. The sponsor doesn't help either; boxed-out on a completely different colour background it makes this whole design a right old mess.
Worn by: Efan Ekoku, Jeremy Goss

'90S MOMENT

It didn't matter what shirt this moment was in, as it remains one of Norwich's greatest nights. The Canaries went to Munich and beat the mighty Bayern in their backyard 2–1 thanks to a Jeremy Goss screamer.

USA 1994

The Americans wanted to come up with something special to celebrate hosting the 1994 World Cup and produced two memorable kits. The home shirt had wavy red stripes that made your eyes go funny, but the away shirt, wow! The denim coloured design used the stars from the national flag to decorate the design, in a winning and very patriotic product from Adidas.
Worn by: Alexi Lalas, Roy Wegerle

EVERTON AWAY 1994/95

The basic colour combination here is good, a nice vibrant 'Everton blue' mixed with black and grey, but it's how it's put together that puts this kit into the decade's crazy category. With two massive panels down each side of the shirt, with zigzag type lines that look like they have been drawn by someone who's used to drawing blueprints rather than football kits. It's made even more fussy by the right panel having an extra strip filled in without the zigzags and just a pale navy. A real 'what were they thinking?' kind of kit.
Worn by: Andy Hinchcliffe, John Ebbrell

CHELSEA AWAY 1995/96

Along with the infamous brown Coventry kit of the late 1970s, the Chelsea away kit of 1995 is up there with the most well-known unusual kit designs. In a perverse way, I kind of like it because it reminds me of a time when kits were at their craziest, but in terms of colours and design it really is a shocker. A combination of granite and bright orange, a colour that should only be twinned with black at best, was merged with a design that included contrasting shades and horrible shoulder panels.

Worn by: John Spencer, David Lee

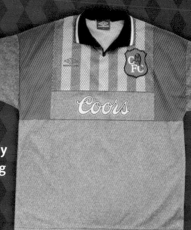

ARSENAL AWAY 1995/96

Gone was the traditional yellow that Arsenal played in away from home, to be replaced by a sleek looking combination of navy and light blue. But this was no normal combination; the lighter blue was actually designed to look like lightning down the right half of the shirt giving it a unique and yet since-repeated design for the Gunners.

Worn by: John Hartson, Paul Merson

'90s MOMENT

Fans turning up late to a 1997 fixture between Coventry and Chelsea may have thought they were seeing the home side taking on the reserves. But in fact, the referee decided the Blues' home shirt clashed with City's and, therefore, Chelsea had to wear Coventry away kits. What, no shirts vs skins?

NOTTINGHAM FOREST AWAY 1995/96

The more you look at this shirt the more you get lost in the detail in what is another classic from the 1990's catalogue. On first glance you'd be forgiven for thinking this was a Watford shirt due to the colour scheme. It's actually a nice shade of yellow and has a smart polo-like collar, but it seems Umbro's design team went a bit art crazy on the shoulders, with a painted Forest mosaic that looked like the badge had been drawn on with an Etch-A-Sketch.

Worn by: Chris Bart-Williams, Steve Chettle

SHEFFIELD WEDNESDAY AWAY 1995/96

These days Puma are one of football's most prominent players, but back in 1995 they were still a long way off the big boys and in their infancy as kit designers. So maybe it explains the horrible design for this Sheffield Wednesday change kit. A base colour that can be best described as 'marine' or dark turquoise is bad enough, but the designers added strange wavy lines halfway down, merging into a darker more navy colour at the bottom of the shirt. Interesting, to say the least.

Worn by: Regi Blinker, Dan Petrescu

ENGLAND GOALKEEPER'S SHIRT 1996

With the world watching, Umbro really wanted England to standout in 1996, and boy did they with the Three Lions' away goalie effort. Decked out in all the colours of the rainbow, this was commonly referred to as 'the refreshers' kit and worn in England's defeat to Germany at Euro '96. Ten out of ten for originality, not quite the same score among fans at the time. I loved it though.

Worn by: David Seaman, Tim Flowers

WORTH A MENTION

Carlisle United
1993
The Confetti

Southend United
1996
The Splat

Hull City
1992
The Tiger

Huddersfield Town
1992
Electric Shock

Newcastle
1997
Mish Mash

7

ON SCREEN

THE MATCH

Live football was a rarity outside the cup finals at the start of the 1990s, except for ITV's *The Match*. Formally called *The Big Match*, it showed a selected number of live games throughout the season from England's First Division. ITV at that time still had the rights to top-flight coverage, having renegotiated a deal with the top ten clubs at the back-end of the 1980s to prevent the BBC and new satellite company Sky from out-bidding them. The show was presented by Elton Welsby and games were commentated by the legendary Brian Moore and backed up by Alan Parry. However, ITV lost rights to the new Premier League in 1992, and the show ended with Liverpool's 2–0 win over Manchester United in 1992, a result that sealed the title for Leeds United.

TELETEXT/CEEFAX

If you couldn't wait to find out the results on *Final Score*, the best and fastest way possible to find the latest footy news in the 1990s was by Teletext. Developed in the 1970s, Teletext was an information retrieval service that sent text and diagrams to your TV through built-in decoders. By the start of the decade it was a standard part of any TV set and used by millions across the country, and football fans relied on it for the latest scores and news. Whether it was Teletext's page 140 or BBC Ceefax's 302, fans would regularly use it to check what was going on during rounds of games. Sometimes it meant waiting for pages and pages to turn before you got to your team, but wait you would, hoping that next time it turned around your team would be ahead. Now very much a thing of the past thanks to the digital takeover, Teletext and Ceefax finally said goodbye to our TV screens in 2012 after slowly being phased out during the 2000s.

GRANDSTAND

Sports fans' weekends began and ended with Grandstand for the majority of the decade – especially football fans. From the opening credits that rung to that familiar theme tune, and Gordon Strachan hitting the goal stanchion right on cue, through *Football Focus* looking at the weekend's action and finishing with the videprinter on *Final Score*, *Grandstand* was sporting utopia on a Saturday.

Football

www.teletext.co.uk/sport

BECKS GETS MADRID MEDICAL ALL-CLEAR 402
Ronaldinho will cost £31m, warn PSG 403
Rovers accept Birmingham's Dunn bid 404
Bellamy hit with racial slur charge 405
Newcastle confirm signing of Bowyer 406
Zola set to return to Italy — agent 407
Five clubs chasing Kewell █ Dacourt 408
Boro hoping to seal Doriva transfer 409
Allardyce rules out swoop for Sukur 410
Li Tie in limbo after loan finishes 411
Fresh Uefa warning for England fans 412

BRIEFS 413 RESULTS/TABLES/FIXTS 415

PAY OFF YOUR DEBTS ! SEE p357

years before the red button was needed. Football fans will particularly remember the videprinter, a digital device that printed out the scores as if somebody was doing it on a typewriter. It meant you were literally waiting on letters to find out the final scores. It was also very surprised when a team scored seven, typing out both the number and then spelling 'seven' out in brackets too. The classified football results were then read out in Len Martin's (and later Tim Gudgin's) own unique way, a tradition the BBC still follows today. Hosted down the years by David Coleman, Des Lynam and Steve Rider *Grandstand* was sadly cancelled in 2007 after nearly a fifty years on air.

SAINT AND GREAVSIE

Cult 1980s football show *Saint and Greavsie* was still going at the beginning of the decade, even if it didn't last long into the 1990s. Presented by former footballers Ian St John and Jimmy Greaves, the show was broadcast at lunchtime on a Saturday afternoon on ITV, as a pre-match warm-up for the day's action. It featured round-ups of goals and reports from clubs around England and Scotland as they looked ahead to the weekend's action. Seen by many as football's first comedy double act, the show was axed in 1992 when the station lost all rights to top-flight football.

SKY SPORTS

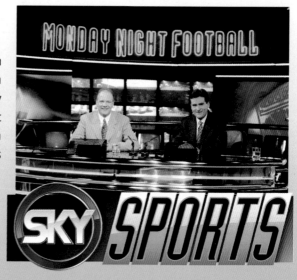

There isn't a single company or product that had a bigger effect on football in the 1990s than Sky and Sky Sports. Its monopoly began right at the start of the decade, when in 1990 satellite company BSB was taken over by the media mogul and millionaire Rupert Murdoch's fledgling company Sky. The takeover meant that from a sports point of view, the new company now had BSB's contacts and emerging talent such as Martin Tyler, former TVAM presenter Richard Keys and ex-footballer Andy Gray. All that was needed to make the new channel, rebranded as Sky Sports, work was a platform – enter the Premier League.

The newly formed top division in the country had broken away from the Football League and was now a solitary entity in its own right. ITV were trying to re-negotiate a deal to keep live top-flight football on the station and were willing to show twenty live games a season with a substantial cash increase for all the top clubs. They were still hopeful of landing the deal right up until decision day, but were blown out of the water by a proposal from Sky that offered £304 million for rights to televise live Premier League football. With that the new kids on the block had won, and league football had been taken off free-to-air television for the very first time.

Sky had their flagship coverage and set about the launch with a campaign entitled *A Whole New Ball Game* that featured adverts with a player from every Premier League club working out, and getting ready for the new season to the theme of Simple Minds' *Alive & Kicking*. Going under the name *Super Sunday*, their coverage kicked-off on 16 August 1992 with Liverpool's trip to Nottingham Forest. Implementing 4 p.m. kick offs to gain more viewers while the terrestrial TV channels still showed religious programmes. With the luxury of time on their side the build-up to the games actually started two hours before and it gave fans an FA Cup final-like build-up to every match, and analysis from the game's biggest names. Another of Sky's earliest innovations was to include the score and clock in the top corner, and that day it saw Teddy Sheringham

score the winner in a 1–0 win for the home side. Following *Super Sunday*, for the first time Sky decided to televise live games on a Monday too, adopting the American tradition of *Monday Night Football*. Debuting at Maine Road, for a clash between Manchester City and Queens Park Rangers, Sky gave the coverage the full razzmatazz, with dancing cheerleaders, parachute jumpers and even giant sumo wrestlers as part of the big match preview. In reality it was an opportunity for the league's lesser-supported clubs to gain a slice of live action in a time-slot not as highly regarded as Sunday's live coverage. It also gave birth to Andy Gray's gadgets and tactical analysis of the game, something which started

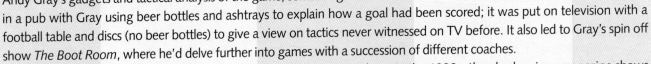

in a pub with Gray using beer bottles and ashtrays to explain how a goal had been scored; it was put on television with a football table and discs (no beer bottles) to give a view on tactics never witnessed on TV before. It also led to Gray's spin off show *The Boot Room*, where he'd delve further into games with a succession of different coaches.

As a dedicated sports channel, it wasn't just live football Sky brought us in the 1990s, they had various magazine shows to back up their unrivalled coverage. *Sky Soccer Weekend* previewed all forthcoming fixtures, with *Goals on Sunday* offering highlights the day after games. *The Footballers' Football Show* dealt with the latest football issues discussed with a panel of pros and journalists. But two other shows launched in the 1990s (and still going today) shaped the way we watched football forever – *Soccer AM* and *Soccer Saturday*. First launched as a breakfast show in 1994 with Russ Williams and starting at the ridiculously early time of 7 a.m., *Soccer AM*'s format changed three years later under the guide of Tim Lovejoy. Lovejoy had previously worked on Channel 4's *The Big Breakfast* and used that model to mix with *Fantasy Football* to produce and present his version of the show, with former kids' presenter Helen Chamberlain, starting at the more reasonable time of 9 a.m. The pair became a popular double act, along with various segments and sketches like *Third Eye*, *Soccer Locker* and the show's variations on shooting a ball through different kinds of holes in walls. It was so popular that footballers often watched it in their hotel rooms before games, and celebrity guests on the show were as high profile as Noel Gallagher and a number of American film stars. Its combination of genuine humour, fan participation and previews of the day's footballing action, meant is has been a winner for Sky for over fifteen years now.

Soccer Saturday evolved from the station's version of *Grandstand*, *Sports Saturday*, when in 1995 the call was made to have the show concentrate on just football. The idea was to have constant updates on scores up and down the country from reporters, and hosted by Jeff Stelling. As well prepared as Stelling was, though, watching one man simply read out scores for several hours was unlikely to make for thrilling television. To this end, he was joined in the studio by a number of former professional players who would watch one of the matches on a monitor in front of them and report on the action. The idea of watching somebody watching television seems ludicrous, but somehow *Soccer Saturday* seemed to work and quickly became cult viewing

among football fans. Stelling's quick wit and good humour undoubtedly played a part, with running gags aimed at Scottish striker Kevin Webster, remarking 'Sally will be pleased' every time he scored, and Welsh side TNS whose goals were always met with, 'They'll be dancing in the streets of Total Network Solutions tonight.' The pundits were also carefully chosen, with George Best and Rodney Marsh always at their outspoken best and Chris Kamara becoming a cult hero for his line 'It's unbelievable Jeff!' For all the fun, though, the information came first, and this was the best place to be if you couldn't get to your team's games.

As Sky entered the new century, their coverage had become unparalleled, with Sky Sports 2 and 3 adding yet more airtime for football and more sports. While the money they were contributing to the game was helping the Premier League become the best in the world, little did we know it was just the beginning and throughout the next decade and beyond, the coverage and innovations would grow and grow to become an everyday part of football fans' lives. They certainly did bring a whole new ball game.

'90s MOMENT

Easily Sky's most famous post-match interview came during Kevin Keegan's reign as Newcastle boss. After taking offence to comments made by rival manager Alex Ferguson, Keegan went on a memorable rant at the Scotsman that repeated the phrase 'I'd love it, I'd love it if we beat them'.

MATCH OF THE DAY

It might be a staple of Saturday night viewing these days, but believe it or not when the decade kicked off, *Match of the Day* was missing from our TV screens. With ITV holding the top-flight rights, *MOTD* was reduced to one off shows and some FA Cup games. That all changed in 1992 when, as part of the BSKYB bid, the BBC acquired the lead highlights package for the all-new Premier League. Hosted by Des Lynam and later Gary Lineker, the show and the most famous theme tune in football returned for the start of the 1992/93 season and would become part of the furniture for the remainder of the decade. Alan Hansen and Mark Lawrenson lead the punditry views behind the desk, while John Motson, the late Tony Gubba and the brilliant Barry Davies provided commentary of the games.

Its popularity saw it become more than a TV show too, with a whole range of merchandise released bearing the name and logo – including this alarm clock that woke you up to *that* theme tune. *Match of the Day* is surely football's most famous show.

FANTASY FOOTBALL LEAGUE

Take two comedians, a sports reporter in a dressing gown, a host of celebrity guests talking football, and what do you have? *Fantasy Football League* that's what. Starting off life as a Radio 5 show playing on the postal game Fantasy Football – where fans picked eleven players from the top flight and gain points from their performances – its success using celebrities in the role of managers led to the BBC adapting the concept for a new TV show. Seeking a new vehicle for David Baddiel after his comedy partnership with Rob Newman had ended, he was teamed up with Frank Skinner, who he'd actually met while watching the football backstage at a gig in 1990, and *Fantasy Football League* was born in January 1994. Kicking off on a late Friday night slot, it soon became obvious that the fantasy game aspect of the show was inferior to Baddiel and Skinner's in-jokes about football and ridicule of current stories. Indeed, the opening section of the show was called *Things We Noticed While Watching Football This Week* and consisted of clips from the previous seven days that the comedians could make fun of. Other memorable sections of the programme included *Phoenix From The Flame*, where a well-known player was invited to recreate a famous moment from their career alongside the pair. In another, ITV was mocked for lack of football coverage in *Saint and Greavsie Talk about the Endsleigh League as if it's Important*. Archived clips were used in other segments such as *Old Football was Rubbish* and *Pele was Shite*.

Each episode also ended with Frank singing an obscure song with his all-time West Bromwich Albion hero, Jeff Astle. Football pundit Angus Loughran completed the line-up as the character Statto, a dressing-gown wearing geek, who used to roll off the Fantasy League numbers while the crowd chanted his name.

It was a show unashamedly aimed at fans, Skinner recalling, 'It was hardcore football fans who were our target audience. We never talked down to them or bothered to explain an obscure football reference. If you didn't know about football, that was tough.' Its success saw the pair included in the Beeb's 1994 World Cup coverage, often wearing ginger wigs and beards to pay homage to USA's Alexi Lalas, and two years later the show enjoyed new heights with Baddiel and Skinner's popularity after the release of *3 Lions*. The show ran from 1994 to 1996 before moving to ITV for live specials and a series throughout the 1998 World Cup.

FOOTBALL ITALIA

'GOOOOOLLLLLLACIO!' was the sound heard on Saturday and Sunday morning thanks to Channel 4's Italian football coverage, most notably *Gazzetta Football Italia*. The move by Channel 4 came after the station had broadcast a documentary showing Paul Gascoigne's return from injury and impending move to Lazio. Afterwards Gazza had said to producer Neil Duncanson that it was a shame British viewers would not be able to see his Serie A games. With that in mind and the league's contract up with SKY, Duncanson saw the opportunity to show one of the best leagues in the world on terrestrial TV, and a deal was struck for Channel 4 to show a live match from Serie A every Sunday afternoon. They showed Sampdoria v Lazio as their first ever live game in September 1992, and it attracted three million viewers.

To accompany the live coverage, a Saturday morning magazine show was also launched called *Gazzetta Football Italia*. Originally the plan was for it to be presented by Gascoigne himself, and although he did appear in various segments the show eventually looked elsewhere for a lead anchor. In James Richardson they found the perfect lead, even if it was by accident. Richardson was working behind the scenes at Channel 4, and hadn't previously worked in front of the cameras. However, due to his fluency in Italian and knowledge of football he was given the nod to front the programme and approached it with a uniquely laid-back and somewhat humorous approach. Regularly presenting the show from outside a pavement café, leafing through Italian newspapers and translating the local stories. Richardson also had the ability to be extremely quick-witted and come up with some memorable lines – once describing a particularly hopeless bottom-of-the-table scrap as featuring 'more errors than a South African archery competition'. He also knew how to be the right kind of light-hearted, for example when he memorably performed the lambada with Attilio Lombardo. With Richardson at the helm for both the weekend's shows, Italian football became a huge success for Channel 4, and the station also went on to cover Italian international games later in the decade.

DO I NOT LIKE THAT

Poor old Graham Taylor, he probably thought it would be a good idea to have a documentary team follow him around to witness a successful bid for World Cup qualification. Unfortunately, with things turning sour on the pitch, what was created turned out to be actually quite the opposite, but made *Do I Not Like That* compulsive viewing for fans. Playing on Taylor's most famous phrase, the documentary is now infamous for showing England's downfall under Taylor and the failure to qualify for USA '94. With Phil Neal emerging as the ultimate yes man, Taylor's insistence on swearing and shouting 'CARLTON!' at the top of his voice, and his own touchline meltdown as a Ronald Koeman-inspired Holland cost him his job, it remains one of the best ever football documentaries.

ALL IN THE GAME

This one-off series from ITV in 1993 was created by England star Gary Lineker and his agent, John Holmes. It was the story of English footballer Darren Matthews (played by Lloyd Owen), who finds himself the UK's biggest export when he signs for Spanish champions Barcelona. Familiar territory for Lineker who made the same move earlier in his career, but i'm sure he didn't have to deal with the same off-the-pitch shenanigans that Matthews does in this largely forgotten drama.

DREAM TEAM

If it's drama you want, then no club in the history of football – and possibly in the history of television – have had more dramatics than Harchester United in Sky One's *Dream Team*. I can hear you already humming the theme tune in your head, and no wonder, *Dream Team* was an essential part of late 1990's viewing on Tuesday and Wednesday evenings. Concentrating on West Midlands football side Harchester United, its run began on 7 October 1997 with the series primarily focusing on the Dragon's youth side and their breakthrough to the first team. The season's first episode set the tone for what was to come, as Dean Hocknell made a goal-scoring debut and then spent the evening celebrating by fooling around with the owner's daughter on his boardroom table. Sky pulled out all the stops for the first season, with Ron Atkinson the club's manager and Derby forward Dean Sturridge joining the show, but it was the memorable characters and outlandish storylines that got fans tuning in – from owners Stephanie Jacobs and Jerry Block to the many players such as Karl Fletcher, Luis Amor Rodriguez and Leon Richards and eye candy like Lynda Block and Kelly James. Of the three seasons that covered the 1990s, perhaps *Dream Team*'s most brilliantly ridiculous moment was when captain John Black took the hitman's bullet intended for Mrs Block, in the midst of Harchester's FA Cup final victory celebrations at Wembley. That's why we loved it!

'90s MOMENT

Somehow *Dream Team* blurred with real-life football in 1999, when the *News of the World* and *The Times* were duped into stating that Liverpool were keen on signing French defender Didier Baptiste. Little did they know they were being hoaxed as Baptiste was actually a fictional character who had just joined the Harchester cast.

RENFORD REJECTS

Children's TV also got its dose of footy fun in the 1990s, with *Renford Rejects*. Produced and broadcast by satellite station Nickelodeon, the story concerned a five-a-side football team made up of players who had been turned down by their school team. They were named Renford Rejects, thanks to a rival sabotaging their league entry form, and included a right rabble of colourful characters. Hull City supporting captain and dreamer Jason, the team's deluded Italian import Bruno Di Gradi, poetry loving Deirdre Barlow look-a-like Ben, wannabe model Ronnie, and the team's secret weapon Robin – the only one with any talent but being a girl wasn't allowed to play for the school team. With Vinnie Rodrigues the aspiring football commentator on the sidelines, its popularity saw a number of guest stars from the world of football appear as themselves, including Ian Rush, Gianfranco Zola, Harry Redknapp and Jim Rosenthal.

THE HURRICANES

A rare animated moment of 1990s nostalgia comes in CITV cartoon caper *Hurricanes*. Boasting a catchy theme tune beginning with 'We're the Hurricanes', the series focused on football team the Hurricanes battling for footballing supremacy over teams from all over the world. From the deep jungles of South America to the busy cities of Moscow and London, the team's enthusiastic 12-year-old owner Amanda and coach Jock led the team through matches against Egyptians, Transylvanians and their ultimate rivals, Gorkos Gorgons. Running from 1993 to 1997, it came at a time when CITV dominated the afternoon TV schedule with some of the most memorable children's shows of that era.

BORN KICKING

A one-off football drama, part of the BBC's 1992 Screen One series, *Born Kicking* posed the question, what would happen if a girl was good enough to play in the professional men's game? The girl in question was Roxy, an intelligent A-level student who abandons her mountain bike outside school to accept a lift from a football club chairman and kick-start her Roy of the Rovers style rise to stardom. Every cheesy cliché is included on the way, from Roxy dolls to appearing in *Hello* and, of course, falling for the married chairman of the club. All set to

the sound of montage classics such as *Holding out for a Hero* and disapproval from the show's most male chauvinistic characters. It wasn't the prettiest of dramas but Roxy had girl power mapped out long before Posh and the rest of the gang arrived.

AN EVENING WITH GARY LINEKER

Starting off life as a stage play, *An Evening with Gary Lineker* was adapted for television ahead of the 1994 World Cup. Set against the backdrop of the 1990 World Cup semi-final between England and West Germany, it featured characters Monica and Bill (played by Caroline Quentin and Clive Owen) on holiday in Ibiza. Bill desperately wants to watch the match, Monica wants to talk about their relationship, and the story is a conflicted mix of both points of view. The ninety-minute drama also starred Martin Clunes, Paul Merton and a cameo from Gary Lineker himself.

MY SUMMER WITH DES

Written by Arthur Smith, one half of the duo that brought the BBC *An Evening with Gary Lineker*, *My Summer with Des* was another one-off footy-themed drama. Starring Neil Morrissey and Rachel Weisz, along with guest appearances from Des Lynam and David Seaman, it is set during the European Football Championships of 1996. Neil plays Martin, a football fan that finds himself out of a job and dumped by his girlfriend, but then bumps into the mysterious Rosie (Weisz). What follows is a romance fuelled by the magical summer of Euro '96, that includes a moment all men dream of: watching England score while reaching happy point with a beautiful naked lady. Screened in the run-up to France 1998, it's a rarely remembered gem of a footy drama.

WHEN SATURDAY COMES

The 1990s may have had wall-to-wall football on the small screen, but it was not until 1996 that *When Saturday Comes* came to the big screen. This Sean Bean-led rags-to-riches tale told the story of Bean's character Jimmy Muir, a factory worker from Sheffield who dreams of playing for local club Sheffield United. Straying from reality at every possible angle, Muir battles his way through a booze habit and the death of his brother to a place in the Blades first team, scoring the winner in an FA Cup semi-final in the film's crescendo. Not the most realistic piece of sporting drama you'll ever see (especially with Bean being 36 when the film was made – not the age of a rookie by a long shot), but enjoyable all the same.

I.D.

Football hooliganism was thankfully something we saw much less of in the 1990s, that is of course unless you happened to be a fan of Shadwell Town. 'Shadwell who?' I hear you ask. Shadwell were the team that 1994 film *I.D.* was built around; however, this movie wasn't about what happens on the pitch, but very much the antics off it. It starred Reece Dinsdale as a cop sent undercover to bring down football gang warfare, only for him to be swallowed up by the hard fighting and hard drinking world of hooliganism to become a Shadwell thug himself. Easily the best film on the subject available, it also features some early appearances from *EastEnders* favourites Billy Mitchell and Dr Truman as part of the Shadwell Army!

VHS

DVD was still some years off for us in this era, so we were still holding our fingers on fast forward and rewind buttons for the majority of the decade. The last big VHS boom did, though, produce some classic footballing collections, which are still being transferred to more modern technology today (or is that just me?). First of which, is a tradition still going strong in today's market, the classic Season Reviews, giving you an excuse every summer to relive whatever happened in your club's previous campaign. These were often backed up by various summaries of the season releases too including 'Goals Galore', 'Saves Galore' and 'Race for the Championship' or later under different name but similar compilations. Then there were two specific releases made in the 1990s, for all twenty of the top-flight clubs, 'The Golden Goals'

collection and 'The Pain and the Glory' series. Each featured memorable moments and goals from clubs' archives, set to popular and sometimes baffling choices of music.

For a more comedic look at football, this era also saw the first release of what is now a standard part of Christmas DVD catalogues – the gaffe videos. The first was presented by Danny Baker and called *Own Goals and Gaffs* and was a rundown of the worst and most humorous moments seen on a football pitch. I can still recall that moment Gary Crosby headed the ball out of Andy Dibble's hands – made me laugh anyway.

WORTH A MENTION

ITV may have lost the top-flight rights in 1992, but they became the go-to station for the newly rebranded Champions League. With Matt Lorenzo, and later Bob Wilson, fronting the coverage, the station aired the cream of Europe and its best competition for the whole of the 1990s. The FA Cup changed stations on a number of occasions, with BBC, Sky and ITV all broadcasting it throughout the decade. But no one did it better than the Beeb, who, in the early 1990s, dedicated entire days worth of schedules to the showpiece event. Channel 5 launched in 1997 and was soon throwing their hat into the football ring by showing UEFA Cup matches, while radio stations such as Capital Gold and Radio 5 kept fans informed of what was going on during match days, and BBC's *Sportsnight* was an added bonus for anything mid-week.

DAVE BUSST

'90s MOMENT

Something which thankfully wasn't shown on live TV was the most horrific injury of the '90s. Coventry City's David Busst sustained compound fractures to both his fibula and tibia during a match with Man Utd in April 1996. The injury was so severe that blood had to be cleaned off the grass, while Peter Schmeichel is said to have vomited on the pitch.

Away from the actual action, football played a part in some of the eras most famous light entertainment shows too. BBC's *A Question of Sport* continued with a regular guest from the world of football, *Spitting Image* on ITV continuously showed up the games biggest characters, and we saw a whole new side to Gary Lineker on comedy panel show *They Think It's All Over*. Film fans also got to see the movie adaptation of beloved book *Fever Pitch*, but more on that later …

8

ADVERTS

There was plenty of football to keep you entertained between programmes in the 1990s, with a whole host of footy themed adverts. Ranging from the ridiculous to the real life and advertising everything from sports companies to cereals, clothing to hair products, the decade really did have some real classics in advertising.

NIKE

Perhaps most fondly remembered, Nike went all out when it came to advertising in this era. The one television advert that's regularly still discussed down the pub today is the Good *vs* Evil campaign from 1997. Pitting a team of the devil's creatures against the game's biggest superstars, it featured Ian Wright arguing with the referee and Eric Cantona flicking up his collar with an 'au revoir' and a winning penalty. The sports brand also produced the Parklife Ad that saw their Nike sponsored athletes compete in a Sunday League battle, and the advert that captured the sizzling skills of Brazil's national team, showboating their way through an airport en route to France '98.

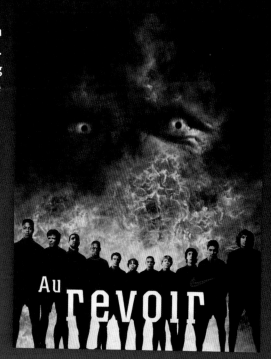

LUCOZADE SPORT

Everyone's favourite get well drink went all sporty during this decade with Lucozade Sport. It produced an advert to launch the new brand that had kids up and down the country trying to recreate it. John Barnes was the star chosen to front it, and it showed him enjoying his new soft drink, then calmly volleying the can into the bin. Never had bins been in more danger from footy fans thinking they could do the same. Alan Shearer would star in a later ad for the drinks company.

TAKE SPORT SERIOUSLY.

PIZZA HUT

Penalty shoot-out defeats are something England fans have become used to, and a post-Euro '96 Tv ad for Pizza Hut saw the funny side of it too. Chris Waddle and Stuart Pearce had been the spot-kick villains from Italia '90, and here they welcomed the summer's newest recruit to the missed penalty club, Gareth Southgate, and shared a famous pizza from one of the world's biggest chains.

WALKERS

Gary Lineker's domination of the 1990s continued with him being the face of Walkers crisps. The Leicester-based company chose the former Leicester City star to front their range of snacks in 1995, and he starred in a variety of adverts throughout the decade. In 1998 Walkers even roped in former England teammate Paul Gascoigne to recreate his famous World Cup tears and launch the 'Salt & Lineker' flavour, and later a young Michael Owen as 'Cheese and Owen' hit the shops.

SKY

We've already touched on Sky's *Alive & Kicking* commercial that launched their coverage of football in this country, however every year their new season adverts became something to look forward to. The best came in 1997 when actor Sean Bean provided a rallying speech on why football mattered. Set against a rousing dance-beat and using clips of the previous season's best moments, Bean told the viewers:

Life, it can be difficult, we all know that. We all need someone to rely on, someone that's going to be there, someone that's going to make you feel like you belong, someone constant. It's ecstasy, anguish, joy and despair. It's part of our history, part of our country and will be part of our future. It's theatre, art, war and love. It should be predictable but never is, it's a feeling that can't be explained, yet we spend our lives explaining it. It's our religion, we don't have to apologise for it, we do not deny it. They're our team, our family, our lives. Football, we know how you feel about it, cos we feel the same.

Now that's a speech.

REEBOK

Reebok's campaigns during this era usually centred around one man, Ryan Giggs, who has worn the brand's boots for his entire football career. While working with the company in the 1990s, Giggs became a flower stall worker in a campaign that also saw Peter Schmeichel as a pig farmer, Dennis Bergkamp as a cheese packer and Andy Cole working in a chip shop. The Welsh star was also among a host of celebrities from that era, including Robbie Williams, Tom Jones and Anna Friel, who dreamt about being in the *This is My Planet* campaign, and in 1997 was turned into plasticine for Reebok's doppelganger advert. Away from Giggs, and as Liverpool's kit supplier in the mid-1990s, Reebok played on the Scouse stereotype with a magazine advert showing a whole stadium in curly wigs and moustaches.

I was about 15 I think. My mum gave me the money to buy some new Reebok football boots. But on the way to the sports shop I decided to get a cheaper pair so I could take a girl to the pictures. *Ryan Giggs. Flower seller. Cardiff, Wales.*

THERE ARE OTHER BOOTS. BUT THEN THERE ARE OTHER CAREERS.

I was going to buy a new pair of Reebok boots. But my friends talked me into buying Woolworths reject. Wasn't it called a Poor group passover? *Andy Cole. Shop group assistant. Nottingham, England.*

THERE ARE OTHER BOOTS. BUT THEN THERE ARE OTHER CAREERS.

I sometimes wonder what I could have achieved if I had bought some good quality Reebok training kit instead of that cheap nylon rubbish. *Peter Schmeichel. Pig farmer. Gladsaxe, Denmark.*

THERE IS NO OTHER KIT. BUT THEN THERE ARE OTHER CAREERS.

It was my 10th birthday. My father gave me a choice. A pair of Reebok football boots or a new train set. I have never regretted taking the train set. *Dennis Bergkamp. Cheese packer. Amsterdam, Holland.*

THERE ARE OTHER BOOTS. BUT THEN THERE ARE OTHER CAREERS.

COCA-COLA

Coke has had a long association with football and can be regularly seen as one of the sponsors of the decade's international tournaments, as well as being attached to the League Cup. It's down to that deal that one of my personal favourite print adverts came about. Using whoever the two teams in the Coca-Cola Cup final were, they changed their famous red cans to the colours of the two sides. Simple but brilliant, it's a shame it was only run for the 1994 and '95 finals. They also did a campaign during the decade using the line, 'Eat Football, Sleep Football, Drink Coca-Cola.'

MCDONALD'S

Scott Parker may now be a full England international with hundreds of Premier League appearances under his belt, but to children of the 1990s, he'll always be that kid from the McDonald's advert. Showing unbelievable skills for a youngster, he showed he was destined for greatness in 1994's show-reel and got us all practising in the playground. Further into the decade, a more established star in the shape of Alan Shearer was seen surprising an autograph-chasing youngster by popping into his local restaurant for a meal deal.

HAIR PRODUCTS

Footballers began to care more and more about their appearance in this decade, and this gave players an opportunity to become the face of well-known beauty products. No surprise that David Ginola and his luscious locks appeared in a campaign for L'Oreal in 1998, while Brylcream cashed-in on David Beckham's emerging popularity by making him the man to re-launch their hair products. More baffling, though, was Wash & Go using Jason McAteer in an ad for their shampoo; something tells me he probably wasn't their first choice.

'90s MOMENT

Ryan Giggs signed off his first decade of football with his best ever goal, skipping through an entire Arsenal defence, before smashing the ball into the roof of the net in 1999's FA Cup semi-final replay.

FOOD AND DRINK

All meals were covered by footballers in this collection of adverts. Kevin Keegan teamed up with the Honey Monster and Sugar Puffs for an ad in 1997, with Glen Hoddle and Brian Clough sharing his breakfast cereal fame by appearing in ads for Shredded Wheat. Ian Wright was in demand by advertisers and was used in a Nescafe print ad, along with his unforgettable dance to the Chicken Tonight theme tune. When Ryan Giggs wasn't starring for Reebok, he was doing ads for Quorn, while Jaffa Cake's Tang Team in a 1998 campaign captured Tony Adams. Rounding off the grocery list was Roy Keane confessing his sins for Snickers and Ron Atkinson dressed in medieval garb for a Carling ad.

'90s MOMENT

Big Ron made the worst possible first impression when appointed Nottingham Forest manager in 1999. As he walked out onto the City Ground pitch for the first time, he took his place in the dugout and posed for the press. Pity it was the away team dugout. Cue strange looks from the Arsenal subs and a big red face for big Ron.

WORTH A MENTION

Alex Ferguson appearing in magazine ads for American Express, David James showing a different side to his game for Armani, a fake football injury in the name of Hamlet, and a bizarre advert for Jiffy condoms that included the main star using the names of England's 1966 squad to prevent his evening's work from finishing – Bobby Charlton honoured with the night's crescendo moment.

9

USA '94

THE TOURNAMENT

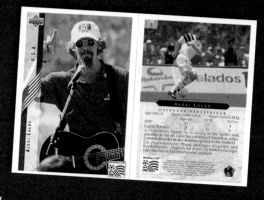

The first World Cup to be held in the land of the free really did have it all – from stars to scandal, tragedy to triumph, and a beginning and an end that had a famous penalty miss. Whereas Italia '90 and Euro '96 are looked on by some (but not this writer) as negative tournaments outside the nostalgic minds of England and Germany, USA '94 and all its razzmatazz is seen as a thoroughly memorable competition only let down by a disappointing and drab final. Yes, England and Scotland weren't there and the kick off times were at an ungodly hour for 1990s kids, but from the moment Diana Ross feebly missed an open goal in the tournament's opening ceremony to the 90,000 plus crowd in the Rose Bowl, this was a World Cup packed-full of incident and top-class football.

The group stage brought a whole host of firsts, for the first ever World Cup in the US of A. The hosts kicked off the tournament against Switzerland by competing in the first finals game to be played under a roof, there were first World Cup goals for Nigeria and Saudi Arabia, and Russia's Oleg Salenko became the first player to score five goals in one match. The early stages weren't without controversy, though, and after scoring in Argentina's first match against Greece, Diego Maradona was sent home after he failed a drugs test. There was also the tragic figure of Andrés Escobar, who was shot dead on returning to Colombia, apparently in retaliation to scoring an own goal in the group match with USA.

On the pitch, there were surprises throughout the early stages, with both Bulgaria and Romania impressing, and Jack Charlton's Republic of Ireland recording a memorable victory over Italy – even if they did spend the rest of the group games arguing over water bottles to deal with the overbearing heat. Brazil and Germany were looking strong in their groups, while Sweden carried on their good form from the Euros to reach the knockout stages.

The Bulgarians' run continued into the round of sixteen where, led by Hristo Stoichkov, they beat Mexico on penalties and then, in one of the tournament's biggest shocks, knocked out Germany thanks to the head of Yordan Letchkov. Italy recovered from their early setbacks to beat both plucky Nigeria and Spain, and Brazil continued to look dangerous thanks to their strike pairing of Bebeto and Romário. They knocked out the hosts and then the Netherlands, in a game that gave the world the 'baby-rocking' celebration. Two tight semi-finals saw Brazil edge past Sweden thanks to another Romário goal and a Roberto Baggio-inspired

Italy put pay to Bulgaria's fairytale World Cup. The final then pitted a Brazil team, who thoug perhaps not the conventional samba style kings we were used to, were equally as effecti against an Italian side led by the divine ponytail. Pasadena's Rose Bowl was sold out witness the final, but unfortunately the teams left their worst performance until la in a forgettable final devoid of any real chances. It meant the World Cup would b decided on penalties for the first time, and with the scores down to 3–2 it was up talisman Baggio to keep Italy's dream alive. However, the Azzurri number 10 blaze the ball over to give Brazil the gong and their first World Cup win since 1970. Wi gates of 3.6 million and more stars than old glory, USA '94 remains one of the mo

THE MASCOT

With the tournament being held in America, it was a no brainer to have a Disney-inspired mascot, and the World Cup's first ever canine. Striker was his name and he was designed by the Warner Bros animation team. Looking every bit like the friendliest dog you've ever seen, the mutt's face was on everything from footballs to badges, glassware and the obligatory cuddly toy.

ENGLAND

It was the first World Cup without England since 1978, and the first without any British representation for twenty-four years. Graham Taylor had continued on as England boss after the disappointing Euro '92 tournament but things had gone from bad to worse for the former Aston Villa manager. Failing to qualify from a group that consisted of the Netherlands, Norway, Poland, Turkey and San Marino, Taylor's England were beaten convincingly in Norway, held by Poland and even managed to let minnows San Marino score past them. The nail in the coffin came in Rotterdam when Ronald Koeman, who should have already been sent-off after a professional foul on David Platt, scored the winner for the Dutch to leave England's campaign in tatters. Taylor, who had cruelly been turned into a turnip by one of the daily newspapers, resigned from his post shortly after the campaign ended and was eventually replaced by Terry Venables. Of the other home nations, it was Wales who came closest to qualifying, losing out on a place only down to a missed penalty from Paul Bodin in their final group game against Romania.

© 1992 ISL

THE RESULTS

Colombia, **Romania**, **Switzerland**, USA

USA	1–1	Switzerland
Colombia	1–3	Romania
Romania	1–4	Switzerland
USA	2–1	Colombia
Switzerland	0–2	Colombia
USA	0–1	Romania

Brazil, Cameroon, Russia, **Sweden**

Cameroon	2–2	Sweden
Brazil	2–0	Russia
Brazil	3–0	Cameroon
Sweden	3–1	Russia
Russia	6–1	Cameroon
Brazil	1–1	Sweden

Bolivia, **Germany**, South Korea, **Spain**

Germany	1–0	Bolivia
Spain	2–2	South Korea
Germany	1–1	Spain
South Korea	0–0	Bolivia
Bolivia	1–3	Spain
Germany	3–2	South Korea

Argentina, **Bulgaria**, Greece, **Nigeria**

Argentina	4–0	Greece
Nigeria	3–0	Bulgaria
Argentina	2–1	Nigeria
Greece	0–4	Bulgaria
Argentina	0–2	Bulgaria
Greece	0–2	Nigeria

Italy, **Mexico**, Norway, **Republic of Ireland**

Italy	0–1	Republic of Ireland
Norway	1–0	Mexico
Italy	1–0	Norway
Mexico	2–1	Republic of Ireland
Italy	1–1	Mexico
Republic of Ireland	0–0	Norway

Belgium, Morocco, **Netherlands**, **Saudi Arabia**

Belgium	1–0	Morocco
Netherlands	2–1	Saudi Arabia
Saudi Arabia	2–1	Morocco
Belgium	1–0	Netherlands
Belgium	0–1	Saudi Arabia
Morocco	1–2	Netherlands

Romania	3–2	Argentina
Saudi Arabia	1–3	Sweden
Netherlands	2–0	Republic of Ireland
Brazil	1–0	USA
Mexico	1–1	Bulgaria (Bulgaria won 3–1 on pens)
Germany	3–2	Belgium
Nigeria	1–2	Italy
Spain	3–0	Switzerland

Romania	2–2	Sweden (Sweden won 5–4 on pens)
Netherlands	2–3	Brazil
Bulgaria	2–1	Germany
Italy	2–1	Spain

Sweden	0–1	Brazil
Bulgaria	1–2	Italy

Sweden 4–0 Bulgaria

Brazil 0–0 Italy (Brazil won 3–2 on pens)

THE STARS

ROMÁRIO

The man who would go on to score over 1,000 goals in his career was at his peak during USA '94. In Carlos Alberto Parreira's largely pragmatic side, he was the star attraction with a dazzle of Brazilian stereotype. Finishing the finals with five goals and the Golden Ball as player of the tournament, his partnership with Bebeto lit up USA '94 and turned Brazil into World Cup winners.

HRISTO STOICHKOV

Bulgaria's greatest ever player was at his absolute best in the United States. Leading the Bulgarian's unlikely charge to the semi-finals, he scored six goals, sharing the Golden Boot with Russian Oleg Salenko, and was instrumental in the side's famous wins over Argentina and Germany.

10

IN PRINT

When you were growing up, you were either a *Match* reader or a *Shoot* reader. Just like any great football rivals on the pitch, these two publications from the two biggest magazine publishing houses in the country, battled for supremacy throughout the decade. Which only meant good things for someone like me, who actually collected both magazines, because they were both top quality reads and an essential part of the 1990s.

MATCH

Kevin Keegan launched *Match* in 1979, and by 1990 it was a standard weekly purchase for any football fan. It was in this decade that the magazine reached its all-time high, and under editor Chris Hunt sales peaked at a record 242,000 in August 1995, thus becoming the biggest selling football magazine in the country. Hunt revamped the mag, giving it a more colourful and pop magazine feel that saw its popularity grow thanks to top-name interviews, posters and fun features – although mascot DJ Bear was binned and later replaced

'90S MOMENT

One of the decade's biggest rivalries was between Manchester United captain Roy Keane and Leeds United (followed by Man City) defender Alf-Inge Haaland. Keane took exception to a tackle from the Norwegian in 1997 that put the midfielder out of action for six months. So Keane returned the 'favour' in 2001 with an x-rated challenge on Haaland, which Keane later admitted was deliberate.

other spin-off gifts and magazines, it's no wonder the magazine is still going strong today.

One of the highs of magazines of this era was getting footballers involved. Famous faces were often seen dressed up in ridiculous garb for features in the era's publications – including customary Santa outfits. Something you seldom seem from today's football stars.

SHOOT

On the opposite side of the pitch, *Shoot* magazine began even further back. First published in 1969 with World Cup winner Bobby Moore gracing the cover, *Shoot* was the most popular football magazine on the market at the start of the 1990s, and its annuals were just as popular. It too had a makeover during this era, producing a more modern and slick looking magazine, while still aiming for football's teenage audience.

With star interviews, posters of the top players and opinion columns from well-known footballers, it was a must-buy weekly read for anyone growing up in the decade. Now, in 2013, the annuals still grace Christmas lists up and down the country.

LEAGUE LADDERS

Easily the most eagerly anticipated free gift of the season, the League Ladders were as big a part of new season tradition as the Charity Shield. First created by *Shoot* and later used by their rivals, the idea was to put the wall-chart up at the start of the season and keep up-to date with the tables using the small team tabs that slotted into slits on the chart, moving the clubs up and down the tables, as and when they needed to be. It

was fiddly, yes, and sometimes meant moving the poster in all kinds of directions to get the slots open, but it didn't stop the excitement of making sure the right teams were in the right leagues. In most cases, though, enthusiasm for the ladders would usually die-down after a couple of months (especially if your own team wasn't doing so well or some of your tabs went AWOL), even when the charts evolved to include monitoring your team's games and line-ups with a range of fancy graphics and charts. But nothing could beat that new-season sensation of seeing the fresh wall-chart adorning your bedroom wall.

SOCCER STARS

A spin-off of *Shoot*, this monthly title played heavily on the posters and illustrations with small fun features in between. Each issue featured pull-out posters of squads, and a front cover pull-out that would have a wonderfully illustrated picture of a player drawn by Stephen Gulbis. He would also pen his artwork to a regular feature when the magazine asked readers to design new kits for teams. Every issue came with a free gift and was hosted by the mag's hairless mascot Ball Boy!

MATCH OF THE DAY

With *Match of the Day* back on our TV screens, thanks to the new deal with BSKYB, BBC magazines saw the chance to expand the brand in 1996 and launched a spin-off magazine under the same title. Taking guise as a weekly publication and aimed at an older audience than some of the current weeklies, its first issue came out in August of that year with David Beckham as their chosen cover star. Using the TV show's pundits as columnists, the magazine was predominately a look back at the previous weekend's games, and a look ahead to upcoming fixtures. It also had selected features, one of which in the first issue was a season preview using football fans as kit models. It later went to a fortnightly schedule and eventually a monthly title before closing in 2001.

90 MINUTES

JULIAN DICKS JOINS EAST 17

90 Minutes arrived on the scene in 1990 and was founded by Crystal Palace fan Dan Goldstein and Paul Hawksbee – now known for his work on talkSPORT. The pair published the magazine themselves before IPC bought the title in 1992 adding it to their football catalogue and giving it to the mainstream. The weekly title reached its peak in the mid-1990s as a slightly more grown up alternative to *Match* and *Shoot*, with longer articles and insider jokes. It was also memorable for its calendars drawn by Nick Davis that showed up footballing personalities as if they were movie stars or famous couples. Perhaps the magazine's biggest claim to fame before it ceased publication in 1997 was its role in the fairytale of one Posh and Becks. It's believed that Victoria Beckham first spotted a picture of young David while doing a famous cover-shoot for *90 Minutes*. Well that's how the story goes anyway.

FOURFOURTWO

Now the UK's biggest selling football magazine, *FourFourTwo* has been going so long that its title is actually out of date in modern football formations. Launched in 1994, with a Terry Venables-led cover, the monthly football magazine was aimed at adults and focused on big, interesting features alongside topical interviews. Columnists on the magazine have included notable journalists such as James Richardson and Henry Winter, while Bobby Robson and Brian Clough also provided content in the 1990s. The magazine's logo also used to include a quote underneath from one of the interviews inside, while the spine line competition asked readers to solve a riddle – something it regularly does today. The magazine celebrated its 200th issue in 2011 and remains the daddy when it comes to footy reads.

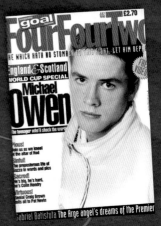

TOTAL FOOTBALL

Offering a slightly more satirical view on football, *Total Football* used elements of the UK's growing 'lads-mag' culture upon its launch in September 1995. 'Total Football is what would happen if you took the brain of the wittiest and SEXY football fan in the world and, using a special machine, turned them into a magazine,' said editor Gary Whitta at the time, and the approach proved to be successful. The first issue featured Ruud Gullit and Dennis Bergkamp on the cover, and the magazine went on to sell around 80,000 copies a month thanks to its mix of naughty jokes and selection of scantily-clad football themed ladies. It ceased publication in 2001, citing the massive expansion of TV, internet and newspaper coverage for its downfall.

ENGLAND MAGAZINE

'Putting the Grr back into Eng-ger-land', this short-lived magazine, solely themed around the national team, was created to cash in on the pre-Euro '96 hype. Issue one hit the stands in June 1995 with 'The Assassin' Alan Shearer on the front cover and featuring interviews with Jamie Redknapp, Darren Anderton and Michelle Gayle (remember her!). With only a selected number of topics to cover, the bi-monthly title only managed a life pan of just over a year before disappearing forever.

WHEN SATURDAY COMES

With fanzines on the rise at football grounds throughout the 1980s, record store assistants Mike Ticher and Andy Lyons took advantage of the growing trend and published a general football fanzine of their own in 1986 called *When Saturday Comes*. It aimed to give a voice to the football supporter who wasn't a hooligan or a racist, nor a knuckle-scraping, train-destroying nitwit, and by the 1990s was a big favourite among fans. So much so, that a leading magazine publisher nearly bought the title during this decade, but the founders decided to uphold their independence and continue in the vein that had made the magazine so popular. Shying away from the latest media outcries, and player interviews centred around a new boot, *WSC*'s thought-provoking and alternative take on football is why the publication is still going today.

THE RED CARD

Mixing the 1990s boom of football publications and a style akin to *Viz*, little remembered *The Red Card* magazine tried to mix fanzine with adult comic without any real success. The launch issue included cover-lines such as 'Do Footie stars shag enough?' and 'Was Stanley Matthews Cack?' and featured comics mocking Alan Hansen, Vinnie Jones and Eric Cantona. It didn't last long, and neither will I talking about it.

LITTLEWOODS POOLS

Predicting football results has never been straightforward, but that didn't stop us (well more likely our dads in this case) trying to pick winners every week to win the Littlewoods Pools game. As big as the National Lottery back in the day, each week you'd stick crosses by those matches you think would end in a score draw and hope that you'd match the weekend's results to nab yourselves the jackpot. It was taken so seriously that even after the classified football results were read out on *Final Score*, you were informed on how the scores had affected the pools picked, and even given a one-word summary of the likelihood of winning. Costing very little to enter, agents went door-to-door collecting entries, and in 1994 a syndicate from Worsley recorded the biggest ever winnings of over £2 million.

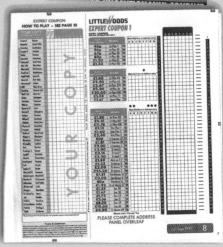

FANTASY FOOTBALL

Despite many believing that the game of Fantasy Football was created thanks to Baddiel, Skinner and the theme their show revolved around, the game actually pre-dates the popular television show and was first played in this country in 1991, by the official Fantasy League game. Having seen the model work in America via the Baseball league, it was adapted for football and run as both a mail order game through *90 Minutes* magazine, and the Radio 5 celebrity game. Its success and exposure saw the *Daily Telegraph* create a newspaper game with the League, gaining over 350,000 entrants from its million readers during its first run in 1994. Two years later the first online games were launched and by then every national newspaper was running their own version of the Fantasy Football concept, including *The Sun*'s 'Dream Team' which became one of the most popular versions of the game, and left me agonising for hours as to why my father continually used to beat me despite me having better players – takes time to realise you need consistent scorers as well as high scorers in this game! Seventeen years on, the official game is still going strong and the concept is a staple of pre-season excitement whichever version takes your fancy.

WORTH A MENTION

Football's longest running magazine remains *World Soccer*. First launched in 1960 it was still going strong in the 1990s and remains a well-respected title in modern day publishing. The decade also saw spin-offs for Match in the guise of *Big Shots*, a poster version of the title to rival *Soccer Stars* and *Sported* – a magazine covering all sports in the style of the weekly football title that sadly only lasted eighteen months.

Goal came as a rival to T*otal Football*, but slowly went and was merged with *FourFourTwo*, before a brief re-emergence at the end of the decade as a teenage title. *Roy of the Rovers* was still going strong at Melchester Rovers via books and one-off publications, and *The Onion Bag* gave *When Saturday Comes* some competition in the fanzine genre of football publications.

Perhaps my favourite printed memento of the 1990s, though, unfortunately remains unfounded, despite desperate searches from its own creators. *The Sun* newspaper's kit posters, that showed off all the new season's designs in graphic form, is something that even after delving into News International's archived files

11

EURO '96

THE TOURNAMENT

Ah, the magical summer of 1996, the weather was fantastic, the soundtrack unforgettable and the football was almost, almost perfect. After the break up of Czechoslovakia and Yugoslavia, a record number of teams had entered qualification for Euro '96, and for the first time the tournament expanded to feature sixteen teams. All sixteen headed to the English shores and were welcomed with an opening ceremony consisting of Simply Red and a patriotic re-enactment of St George slaying the dragon. When all that fun was over, England kicked off the tournament with a rather disappointing 1–1 draw with Switzerland, but would later make up for it with some fine performances against Scotland and the Netherlands.

In Group B, Bulgaria and Romania failed to live up to their USA '94 reputations and were roundly seen off by France and Spain. Group C produced the early stage's biggest upset, as World Cup runners-up Italy crashed out of the tournament despite winning their opening game against Russia. The Italians' attacking frailties were exposed, as they failed to beat both Germany and the Czech Republic who progressed instead. In the final group, Denmark's defence of the trophy was quickly over as Portugal and a Davor Šuker-inspired Croatia made the knockout stage.

The quarter-finals proved to be tight affairs with half the games going to the dreaded penalty shoot-outs. Clarence Seedorf's missed spot-kick saw France dispatch Holland, while England prevailed over Spain. Elsewhere Karel Poborský notched a memorable winner at Villa Park to see off Portugal and Germany were too strong for the impressive Croats. Two more shoot-outs were needed in the semi-finals, Germany ended England's dream after a 1–1 draw at Wembley, and in the other game France and the Czech Republic failed to get a shot on target in 120 minutes, with the Czechs being victorious in the spot-kick battle. Wembley hosted the final without England, but with two teams who actually met in the opening game of their group stage. It was the Czech Republic who sprung another surprise when Patrik Berger converted a second half penalty to put them in the lead. However, German substitute Oliver Bierhoff equalised minutes after coming on to take the game to extra time, where UEFA's new 'golden goal' rule came into play as Bierhoff struck again to give Germany the trophy.

THE MASCOT

The 1966 World Cup brought football its first ever mascot in World Cup Willy, so thirty years later who better to represent Euro '96 than another king of the jungle – Goliath. Looking fiercer, yet ever more friendly than his famous predecessor, England's fourth lion always had a big smile on his face and wore the team colours with pride.

ENGLAND

Having made little impression four years earlier, and then failing to qualify for USA '94, England's fans were chomping at the bit for Euro '96 and to see what Terry Venables' side could do. Venables had assembled a talented squad; Alan Shearer was now the country's leading marksmen despite the current international goal drought, with a midfield of talent and guile to back him up that included a rejuvenated Gazza. In David Seaman they had one of the world's best goalies and a defence of steel and substance led by Tony Adams. The tournament didn't begin in the best light, however, with newspapers reporting on the player's drunken behaviour on a warm-up tour, including images of some involved in a 'dentist chair' drinking game.

When the action got underway at a sunny Wembley, it was Shearer who ended his thirteen-match barren run to open England's tournament. But a handball from Stuart Pearce in the second half led to a Swiss penalty and meant honours were shared. A week later they met auld enemies Scotland in a highly anticipated clash, that was settled in the second half with a Shearer header and one of Wembley's truly great goals from Paul Gascoigne – backed up with a dentist chair celebration for the tabloids. That win put England in the ascendancy and in their final group game produced the best performance from an England side since 1966, beating one of the tournament favourites, the Netherlands, 4–1 with goals from Shearer and Sheringham. The Patrick Kluivert consolation unfortunately eliminated Scotland. By now Venables had captured the hearts of the country and, backed by the sounds of Baddiel and Skinner, the Three Lions rode their luck in the quarter-final match against Spain, before winning a memorable shoot-out. David Seaman was the hero with some world-class stops, while Pearce exorcised his Italia '90 demons and secured the iconic image of Euro '96 with his celebration.

Wembley then braced itself for another meeting with Germany, and another full of incident. England, in their unusual change strip of indigo blue, made the perfect start when Shearer nodded in after just three minutes. However, they were pegged back on the quarter of an hour mark thanks to a Stefan Kuntz equaliser. From then on England just couldn't find a way through, Darren Anderton hit the post and Gascoigne was inches from a Shearer cross, but the game went to penalties once again. Ten spot-kicks later and the teams were all square, when Gareth Southgate stepped up to become England's unfortunate fall guy. Listen carefully and you'll still be able to hear Barry Davies shout, 'Oh no' even to this day. It was a memorable summer, where England went so far but just not far enough once again.

1	David Seaman	GK
2	Gary Neville	DF
3	Stuart Pearce	DF
4	Paul Ince	MF
5	Tony Adams	DF
6	Gareth Southgate	DF
7	David Platt	MF
8	Paul Gascoigne	MF
9	Alan Shearer	FW
10	Teddy Sheringham	FW
11	Darren Anderton	MF
12	Steve Howey	DF
13	Tim Flowers	GK
14	Nick Barmby	MF
15	Jamie Redknapp	MF
16	Sol Campbell	DF
17	Steve McManaman	MF
18	Les Ferdinand	FW
19	Phil Neville	DF
20	Steve Stone	MF
21	Robbie Fowler	FW
22	Ian Walker	GK

Group A

England, Netherlands, Scotland, Switzerland

England	1–1	Switzerland
Netherlands	0–0	Scotland
Switzerland	0–2	Netherlands
Scotland	0–2	England
Scotland	1–0	Switzerland
Netherlands	1–4	England

Group B

Bulgaria, **France**, Romania, **Spain**

Spain	1–1	Bulgaria
Romania	0–1	France
Bulgaria	1–0	Romania
France	1–1	Spain
France	3–1	Bulgaria
Romania	1–2	Spain

Group C

Czech Republic, Germany, Italy, Russia

Germany	2–0	Czech Republic
Italy	2–1	Russia
Czech Republic	2–1	Italy
Russia	0–3	Germany
Russia	3–3	Czech Republic
Italy	0–0	Germany

Group D

Croatia, Denmark, **Portugal**, Turkey

Denmark	1–1	Portugal
Turkey	0–1	Croatia
Portugal	1–0	Turkey
Croatia	3–0	Denmark
Croatia	0–3	Portugal
Turkey	0–3	Denmark

Quarter-finals

France 0–0 Netherlands (France won 5–4 on pens)

Czech Republic 1–0 Portugal

Spain 0–0 England (England won 4–2 on pens)

Germany 2–1 Croatia

Semi-finals

France 0–0 Czech Republic

(Czech Republic won 6–5 on pens)

England 1–1 Germany

(Germany won 6–5 on pens)

Final

Czech Republic 1–2 Germany (aet)

THE STARS

KAREL POBORSKÝ

The tournament's surprise package, the Czech Republic, had a number of stars, but none shone brighter than Karel Poborský. His looped volley against Portugal was one of the goals of the tournament, and, off the back of Euro '96, he was named Czech Player of the Year and secured a move to Manchester United.

KAREL POBORSKY

DAVOR ŠUKER

After netting twelve goals in ten games during qualifying, Davor Šuker scored three more times at the Euros to show the world his striking ability. His chip over Peter Schmeichel in Croatia's 3–0 win over Denmark is still one of the best goals scored at European Championships. His performances saw him move to Real Madrid that summer, and he later enjoyed a spell at Arsenal.

12

COLLECTIONS

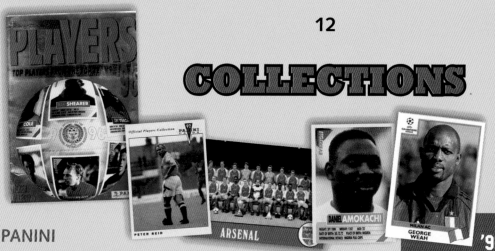

PANINI

No tournament fever was ever complete without the official sticker book and during the 1990s it was Panini who got us all collecting those World Cup and European collections. Established in the 1960s, Panini had become synonymous with our parents when it came to sticker swapping in schools and completing albums. The Italian-based company began this decade with the collection for the 1990 World Cup, and had hold of the domestic market too, with the Football '90–'92 sticker collections and Panini '92 trading card set. By the middle of the decade, they had lost the rights to top-flight football but still produced collections for USA '94 and World Cup '98, the Scottish Premier League, Champions League albums and one-off SuperPlayer sticker collections in both 1996 and 1998. Often seen as a true nostalgic trip for generations before and after the one we are celebrating, Panini remain a worldwide success today.

'90s MOMENT

George Weah may have been one of the world's best during this era, but his 'cousin' is not fondly remembered at Southampton. In truth, Ali Dia was no more related to Weah than you or I, but it didn't stop him blagging a trial at The Dell using the Libyan's name. Five minutes into his debut it was clear Dia had never been near a football pitch and his Saints career lasted just fifty-three unforgettable minutes.

MERLIN

Go to any playground during the Premier League era, and you'd hear the words 'Got, got, got, NEED!' shouted by groups of boys up and down the country. Why? Because they were swapping Merlin stickers, that's why. Having acquired the rights to produce the Premier League collection, Merlin released its first sticker album in 1994. The instant success of the collection took even the publishers by surprise and several re-prints of the album were needed of the first collection that saw Ryan Giggs and Paul Merson grace the cover (one that this author proudly completed, too). What made the collection so popular wasn't just the stickers of players, but Merlin had gone all out with sections on kits, programmes and even a pull-out section on Sky Sports that included a rare sticker of John Salako and Anna Walker looking very 1990s.

The collections continued annually from that point, but Merlin didn't stop at just stickers. They also produced several trading card collections throughout the decade, from the Premier Gold and Ultimate Gold Collections, to pop up and

cartoon cards as part of their Premier League collection. They also cashed-in on a rare 1990s phenomenon, 'pogs', small round cardboard discs that were used as part of a playground game, and Merlin gave them the Premier League makeover too. By the end of the decade, Merlin had been bought out by American company Topps, but still produced all Premier League collections and today are responsible for Match Attax cards, the leading collectable card collection for kids … and some adults.

A rare card collection from before Merlin's Premier League range, Shooting Stars cards were released for the 1991/92 season and featured all the teams from the top flight, and came in a basic looking but handy binder to keep them in. Topps, meanwhile, before buying-out Merlin in 1995, released their own range of trading cards three years earlier called 'Topps Stadium Club'.

PROSET

A popular card collection from 1991, Proset was unique as not only did it cater for the top flight, but also included players from all four leagues. Different colour themes separated the divisions – in descending order red, blue, yellow and some with a greeny turquoise effect. Quantity of cards did decrease as you went down the leagues, but it was here you'd now find some real gems like Dion Dublin at Cambridge or Bristol Rovers' Ian Holloway. The cards also contained wonderfully descriptive paragraphs on their reverse, giving that added bit of information.

To keep your cards together there was a flash binder that was adorned by the England national team logo, not the easiest thing to lug around but it made the collection look all the more stylish. The American based company only ventured into the football market for two seasons before losing the card rights due to the launch of the Premier League; it does, however, remain a smart, memorable collection.

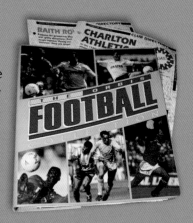

A weekly magazine and football encyclopaedia that gave us two bumper binders of information during its early 1990s run. Designed so that every week you built up the folders page-by-page, the collection had numerous different sections all packed full of football goodness. There was an A–Z guide to every team in the English and Scottish football league, a look back at the great players, matches and goals of the game – including detailed diagrams – and a sticker collection that was unusually set out in order of players' positions. For any statistically hungry kid at the time, with an unhealthy appetite for the game, this was a gold mine of football info, and a never repeated style of collection.

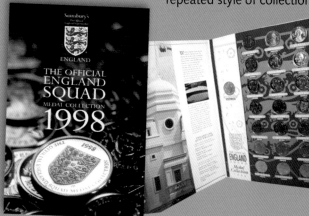

COIN COLLECTIONS

Petrol prices these days mean you're never likely to leave forecourts with more coins than you came in with, but during the 1990s that wasn't the case thanks to these collections. As part of the celebrations for World Cup 1990 an official coin set was released at Esso petrol stations featuring silver coins of the national team squads of England and Scotland, complete with collector's box. Six years later supermarket chain Sainsbury's repeated the collection as part of Euro '96 and then France '98, this time around sticking to just the Three Lions, and producing a booklet that had an inside back-cover full of round holes for your coins.

UPPER DECK

USA's staging of the World Cup finals gave Upper Deck the opportunity to enter the football trading card world for the first time. One of American's leading brands, having catered for the Baseball and the NHL, they produced a brilliantly diverse range of cards for their USA '94 collection. As well as cards of all the star performers, there were also shots of players off the pitch, including Alexi Lalas busting a tune off his guitar, and 'Postcards from Pasadena' for those who didn't qualify, with one card featuring England's David Platt chilling on a beach with a surfboard.

'90s MOMENT

Mexico's Jorge Campos made his name at the 1994 World Cup for his amazingly colourful goalkeeper kits – that he designed himself. He also spent some games as an outfield player as shown by this trading card.

FUTERA

A rare collection that came right at the back end of the decade, and oddly only focused on certain teams. Arsenal, Aston Villa, Celtic, Chelsea, Leeds, Liverpool, Manchester City, Manchester United and Newcastle all got the Futera treatment. Different collections included Masters, Sharpshooters, Fans Selections and a wrath of others from 1998 and 1999.

FOOD AND DRINK

You couldn't delve into sweets, crisps or even tea in the 1990s without finding some kind of football memorabilia. Panini jumped on the pog bandwagon in 1996, giving away discs featuring stars of the tournament in packs of Snickers. Two years later, and to celebrate the 1998 World Cup, PG Tips returned to the football world with their own range of trading cards featuring the biggest stars in the world. Golden Wonder also released their collection called 'Word Cup Shields', a newly shaped football card that slotted ever so nicely into a cardboard folder provided by the crisp maker. Golden Wonder's Wotsits brand also gave us 'wooshers' in packs around this time, which were a mix of a pog keenie and collector medals. Not sure anyone knew what to actually do with them, though. Lastly, Wagon Wheels gave away football trading cards in their packs, both in their 1997 Skills Cards range and World Cup versions a year later, along with Bassett who also produced trading cards in their sweet packets too.

ENGLAND PHOTO ALBUM

A World Cup 1998 collection that was a step away from the stickers or cards and onto something a little bigger – photos. Featuring all the names from England's 1998 squad, they came in squad shots, action poses and images from training. All were kept in a small binder that was much lighter and more compact than used in previous collections. Like a photo album you kept of your family and friends, only with potential World Cup winners instead.

BP ENGLAND CARDS

More football fun from a petrol station came in the guise of BP's Team England Card Collection. Based on the classic cigarette cards of the 1960s, you were given these illustrated collectables whenever you spent over £10 in a BP garage. They even provided a booklet for the cards to go in; unfortunately the sticking in was down to you and therefore it was vital to find the best, non-messy glue to keep your album looking top notch.

NETBUSTERS

'Football's essential monthly video' it was called, and since it was football's only monthly video it was probably right. NetBusters hit shops in March 1995, and was a magazine in video format that featured all the latest football action and behind the scenes footage from the game's biggest stars. Lasting just under an hour, segments included Paul Elliot's Soccer Academy, Dean Holdsworth on Street Soccer and a look at how football boots were invented, and all was presented by Julia Bradbury – well known at the time for her work on *GMTV* and *Wish You Were Here* – and some bloke called Simon Powell (yes, I said Powell, not the other bloke who was busy with Zig and Zag). There were six 'issues' of NetBusters but the seventh never materialised and the magazine show was gone from our video recorders forever.

FOOTBALL MAGIC

Right at the end of the decade a rare collection was released called Football Magic. No, it wasn't a joint venture between Alex Ferguson and Paul Daniels, but a collectable series in the vein of Orbis' version years before. Each week you'd fill your little red binder with new content for sections that included team guides, heroes from the past and football tips to the extent that the collection eventually spread over several binders.

PROMATCH

A card collection unlike any other, ProMatch cards dispensed with the action shots we were used to seeing on cards and gave us a collection we'd never forget. Each card was illustrated with a brilliant looking caricature of a top-flight football star, and was first released in the UK in 1996. Each cartoon-like card had its own unique personality, some were perhaps not as flattering as others but it made the collection a must-have item of the era. There were three domestic collections and two international sets released, as well as two books full of the cards' comical drawings.

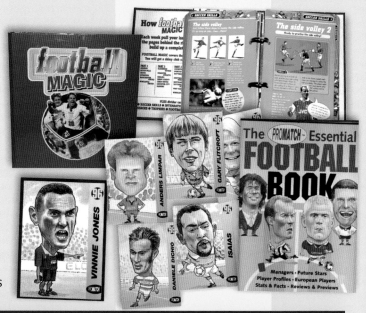

'90s MOMENTS

Not many footballers can lay claim to transferring their 'talents' to the big screen, but in 1998 Vinnie Jones did just that – and it wasn't even a footballing inspired film. After retiring from the game, Jones scored a part in the 1998 Brit gangster flick *Lock, Stock & Two Smoking Barrels* and then went on to forge an impressive movie career.

13

PLAYERS

PAUL GASCOIGNE

Gazza-mania was born and bred in the 1990s. From the moment he Cruyff-turned two Dutch defenders to his tears in Turin, Paul Gascoigne was a bona fide star of the decade. On the pitch he was instrumental in Spurs' FA Cup run of 1991, even ignoring his heart-breaking injury in the final, loved in Italy with Lazio, and Player of the Year while at Rangers. Off it he may have been full of controversy, but he was a genius once he laced up his boots, and his defining moment came at Euro '96 and that goal against Scotland. There really has only ever been one Gazza, and he is seen here as a pin badge from the 1993 set of Superstar Soccer Pins.

RYAN GIGGS

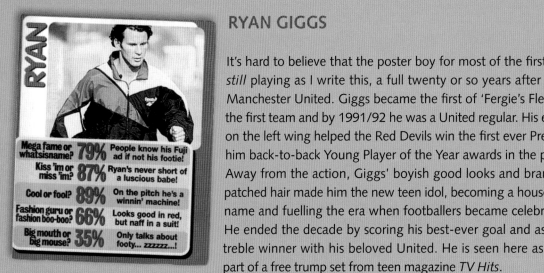

Mega fame or whatsisname?	**79%**	People know his Fuji ad if not his footie!
Kiss 'im or miss 'im?	**87%**	Ryan's never short of a luscious babe!
Cool or fool?	**89%**	On the pitch he's a winnin' machine!
Fashion guru or fashion boo-boo?	**66%**	Looks good in red, but naff in a suit!
Big mouth or big mouse?	**35%**	Only talks about footy… zzzzzz…!

It's hard to believe that the poster boy for most of the first half of the decade is *still* playing as I write this, a full twenty or so years after making his debut for Manchester United. Giggs became the first of 'Fergie's Fledglings' to break into the first team and by 1991/92 he was a United regular. His electric pace and tricks on the left wing helped the Red Devils win the first ever Premier League, earning him back-to-back Young Player of the Year awards in the process.

Away from the action, Giggs' boyish good looks and bramble-patched hair made him the new teen idol, becoming a household name and fuelling the era when footballers became celebrities. He ended the decade by scoring his best-ever goal and as a treble winner with his beloved United. He is seen here as part of a free trump set from teen magazine *TV Hits*.

ALAN SHEARER

Southampton, Blackburn and Newcastle all benefitted from big Al's scoring exploits during the 1990s. Easily the decade's most deadly marksmen, he became British football's most expensive player twice with his £3.2 million move to Rovers and £15 million return to Tyneside in 1996. Shearer collected his only major honour in 1995, winning the Premier League with Blackburn, but remains, at the time of writing, the Premier League's record goalscorer with 260. On the international stage, he became England's number one frontman after making a goal-scoring debut in 1992, won the Golden Boot at Euro '96 and was captain for the World Cup two years later. He is seen here as a rare doll from Hasbro Action range.

MATT LE TISSIER

A scorer of great, great goals, Le Tissier spent his entire career at Southampton but his talent warranted a bigger stage. Whether it was his 40-yard screamer against Blackburn, the flicked free kick at The Dell or the hat-trick of memorable goals he put past Newcastle, Matt's special talent monopolised Goal of the Month charts throughout the decade, without ever getting the international recognition he deserved. A winner of the PFA Young Player of the Year award in 1990, Matt spent the whole of the decade lighting up The Dell, where he was simply known as 'Le God'. He is seen here as a trading card from Bassett.

PETER SCHMEICHEL

Alex Ferguson's best ever buy? It could be argued so. Peter Schmeichel was signed by Manchester United for just £500,000 in 1991, and went on to become not only the best keeper in the world, but one of the best of all time. He was a star for Denmark in their Euro '92 triumph and the backbone for a United team that won it all during this decade. He ended his Red Devils career and the 1990s on the highest note, by winning the Champions League as part of the club's historic treble. He is seen here as a ProMatch coin from their medallion series.

IAN WRIGHT

Ian Wright, Wright, Wright, began the decade by announcing himself on the biggest stage of all – the FA Cup final. He scored twice as Crystal Palace fought out a pulsating draw with Manchester United in 1991's final, before they lost the replay. Wright moved to Arsenal the following season, and it was here that he would become a club legend, scoring a hat-trick on his league debut and winning an FA Cup and League Cup double in 1993. By 1997, Wright had cemented his status as the Gunners' greatest ever goalscorer by breaking Cliff Bastin's record Arsenal haul, and had helped the club win their first Premier League trophy. He is seen here as a phone card available in Asia.

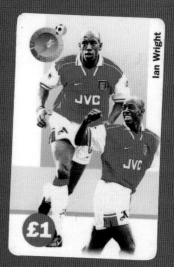

ERIC CANTONA

Lauded as the final part of United's Premier League-winning jigsaw, King Eric built a throne at Old Trafford that he'll never come down from. Kicking off the decade with a League Championship win at Leeds United, Cantona moved to Old Trafford in 1992 and revitalised their season by leading them to their first title for twenty-six years. He was the catalyst for United's dominance of the next decade, and while never short of controversy or arrogance, the maverick Frenchman was a joy to watch on a football pitch. The only disappointment is that he ended his career so early, in 1997, at the age of 30. He is seen here as part of the Flippz motion picture flick-books.

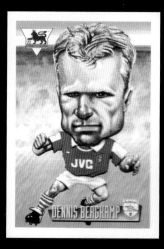

DENNIS BERGKAMP

English football saw many foreign imports hit these shores, as the Premier League became a stronger and stronger force, but none were better than Dennis Bergkamp. Already a Dutch international with a huge reputation, Bergkamp arrived at Highbury in 1995 and enjoyed the peak of his stellar professional career while at the North London club. Instrumental in Arsenal's league and cup double of 1998, he was named PFA Player of the Year, FWA Footballer of the Year and his goal against Leicester best goal of the campaign. He may have hated flying, but we loved watching him play. He is seen here as an illustrated card from Merlin's 1998 set.

DAVID BECKHAM

Few would have foreseen what a global icon David Beckham would become when he made his debut for Manchester United against Brighton in 1994; what was never in doubt, though, was his football talent. Two years later he was lobbing Neil Sullivan from inside his own half and from that point on Beckham's popularity went into overdrive, both with football fans and, thanks to his relationship with Posh Spice, non-football fans alike. 1998's World Cup sending off may have been a low point, but it was far out-weighed by the 90s highs. And that was very much just the beginning for brand Beckham. He is seen here as a doll from Hasbro's Heroes of the Treble range.

MICHAEL OWEN

Michael only arrived on the scene in 1997, marking his Liverpool debut with a goal against Wimbledon, but in just those two and a half years he became an international star. His goals the following season earned him an England call-up, and inclusion to Glen Hoddle's France '98 squad. It was here that Owen made the world sit up and take notice with his mazy run through the Argentine defence, to score one of England's greatest goals. That wonder goal sparked fame both on and off the pitch and set the tone for what was to come. He is seen here as the face of his own computer game.

WORTH A MENTION

Liverpool goal-machine Robbie Fowler, christened 'God' by The Kop; the driving force in Manchester United's midfield Roy Keane; Gary Lineker for both his on and off pitch contributions to the decade; and, skipper for club and country, Tony Adams.

14

FRANCE '98

THE TOURNAMENT

France '98 was the biggest ever World Cup, with thirty-two teams competing, and kicked off unusually with the holders instead of the hosts at Paris' brand new 80,000-seater stadium Stade De France. After the obligatory opening ceremony – one that actually began the night before with giant robots meeting from four sides of Paris – it got underway as reigning champions Brazil beat a stubborn Scotland side en route to topping Group A. The French

began their campaign with a comfortable win over South Africa, and won the group with three wins out of three. Germany, Italy and Argentina also progressed from the group stage as winners and with little trouble. Romania surprisingly finished above England in Group G, while Nigeria were the biggest shock, finishing ahead of Paraguay and seeing Spain and Bulgaria eliminated at the first hurdle. Thankfully the politically charged meeting between the USA and Iran survived without any off-field talking points.

The knock-out stages saw thumping 4–1 wins for Brazil over Chile, with Ronaldo scoring twice, and Denmark who ended Nigeria's good early run. Italy and the Netherlands bested Norway and Yugoslavia, Argentina won the tournament's

first penalty shoot-out over England, and the hosts needed extra time and a Laurent Blanc goal to see off Paraguay. France's luck continued into the quarter-final, as they got the better of Italy in a nail-biting penalty shoot-out where Dino Baggio echoed his namesake with the vital miss. Brazil won an entertaining encounter with Denmark, Dennis Bergkamp helped settled the Netherlands' win over Argentina with another classic goal from his repertoire, and Croatia comfortably knocked-out Germany in one of the results of the tournament, Davor Šuker once again proving his worth on the international stage. Brazil needed penalties to see off the Dutch in the semi-finals, and France turned to an unlikely hero in Lilian Thuram who scored both goals to see off Croatia, and set up a final that would see the tournament's hosts take on the holders.

The game's pre-match build-up was dominated by the omission of Ronaldo from the Brazil line-up after suffering from an alleged seizure, only for him to be reinstated forty-five minutes before kick off. Once on the field the striker did manage to create the first chance, dribbling past Thuram and forcing Fabian Barthez into a save; however, from that point France took over, led by their talisman Zinedine Zidane. The French master's two headed goals settled the tie, and there was still time for Emmanuel Petit to round off a resounding victory and see France crowned World Champions for the first time.

THE MASCOT

French football fans were fully involved in the creation of World Cup '98's mascot, Footix, winning a battle with five other options to be the tournament's representative. Supporters felt that having a cockerel immediately screamed 'French' and was decked out in the country's colours just in case it wasn't clear. The name Footix was chosen by TV viewers and is a portmanteau of 'football' and 'ix' from the popular French comic strip *Asterix*.

ENGLAND

England literally shed sweat and blood to get to France '98, with Paul Ince's red-soaked bandages in the 0–0 draw with Italy a symbol of their qualification campaign. Glenn Hoddle was now the man in charge of the Three Lions, and he picked a squad that included the bulk of Euro '96's heroes, but added a touch of youthful exuberance with the emerging talents of David Beckham, Paul Scholes and 18-year-old Michael Owen. Alan Shearer was now the nation's skipper, but there was no place in the twenty-two for Paul Gascoigne, who allegedly trashed the manager's meeting room upon hearing of his exclusion.

Drawn in a group with Tunisia, Romania and Colombia, they began their campaign against the African's in Marseille with a 2–0 victory thanks to strikes from Shearer and Scholes. The good start was quickly undone in the second match, however, when Dan Petrescu scored a late winner for Romania to take the shine off Michael Owen's first World Cup goal. The passage through the second round was secured with a win over Colombia that included David Beckham's maiden England free kick. Results meant Hoddle's men finished second in the group and set up a mouth-watering tie with Argentina that would be full of controversy. Two penalties inside ten minutes got the game off to a pulsating start, with Gabriel Batistuta and Shearer netting for either side. Then on the quarter of an hour mark, Owen picked up the ball on the halfway line, and in one mazy run and goal later confirmed himself as the future of England's strike-force with one of the World Cup's greatest goals. Javier Zanetti got Argentina back into it just before the break, then David Beckham needlessly kicked-out at Diego Simeone which saw him receive a controversial red card, handing the advantage to the South Americans. England dug deep though, and took the game to extra time and almost snatched it through Sol Campbell's disallowed goal – however, it would go down to penalties once again. This time it was Paul Ince and David Batty who were the fall guys, and England's tournament was over once again thanks to spot-kick heartache. The press blamed one man instead though, Mr Beckham, with a certain newspaper following up the events with the headline 'TEN BRAVE LIONS, ONE STUPID BOY'.

1	David Seaman	GK
2	Sol Campbell	DF
3	Graeme Le Saux	DF
4	Paul Ince	MF
5	Tony Adams	DF
6	Gareth Southgate	DF
7	David Beckham	MF
8	David Batty	MF
9	Alan Shearer (c)	FW
10	Teddy Sheringham	FW
11	Steve McManaman	MF
12	Gary Neville	DF
13	Nigel Martyn	GK
14	Darren Anderton	MF
15	Paul Merson	MF
16	Paul Scholes	MF
17	Rob Lee	MF
18	Martin Keown	DF
19	Les Ferdinand	FW
20	Michael Owen	FW
21	Rio Ferdinand	DF
22	Tim Flowers	GK

THE RESULTS

Group A
Brazil, Morocco, **Norway**, Scotland

Brazil	2–1	Scotland
Morocco	2–2	Norway
Scotland	1–1	Norway
Brazil	3–0	Morocco
Brazil	1–2	Norway
Scotland	0–3	Morocco

Group B
Austria, Cameroon, **Chile**, **Italy**

Italy	2–2	Chile
Cameroon	1–1	Austria
Chile	1–1	Austria
Italy	3–0	Cameroon
Italy	2–1	Austria
Chile	1–1	Cameroon

Group C
Denmark, **France**, Saudi Arabia, South Africa

Saudi Arabia	0–1	Denmark
France	3–0	South Africa
South Africa	1–1	Denmark
France	4–0	Saudi Arabia
France	2–1	Denmark
South Africa	2–2	Saudi Arabia

Group D
Bulgaria, **Nigeria**, **Paraguay,** Spain

Paraguay	0–0	Bulgaria
Spain	2–3	Nigeria
Nigeria	1–0	Bulgaria
Spain	0–0	Paraguay
Nigeria	1–3	Paraguay
Spain	6–1	Bulgaria

Group E
Belgium, **Mexico**, **Netherlands**, South Korea

South Korea 1–3 Mexico
Netherlands 0–0 Belgium
Belgium 2–2 Mexico
Netherlands 5–0 South Korea
Netherlands 2–2 Mexico
Belgium 1–1 South Korea

Group F
Germany, Iran, USA, **Yugoslavia**

Yugoslavia 1–0 Iran
Germany 2–0 USA
Germany 2–2 Yugoslavia
USA 1–2 Iran
USA 0–1 Yugoslavia
Germany 2–0 Iran

Group G
Colombia, **England**, **Romania**, Tunisia

England 2–0 Tunisia
Romania 1–0 Colombia
Colombia 1–0 Tunisia
Romania 2–1 England
Colombia 0–2 England
Romania 1–1 Tunisia

Group H
Argentina, **Croatia**, Jamaica, Japan

Argentina 1–0 Japan
Jamaica 1–3 Croatia
Japan 0–1 Croatia
Argentina 5–0 Jamaica
Argentina 1–0 Croatia
Japan 1–2 Jamaica

Second Round

Brazil	4–1	Chile
Nigeria	1–4	Denmark
Netherlands	2–1	Yugoslavia
Argentina	2–2	England (Argentina won 4–3 on pens)
Italy	1–0	Norway
France	1–0	Paraguay (aet)
Germany	2–1	Mexico
Romania	0–1	Croatia

Quarter-finals

Brazil	3–2	Denmark
Netherlands	2–1	Argentina
Italy	0–0	France (France won 4–3 on pens)
Germany	0–3	Croatia

Semi-finals

Brazil	1–1	Netherlands (Brazil won 4–2 on pens)
France	2–1	Croatia

Third Place play-off

Netherlands 1–2 Croatia

Final

Brazil 0–3 France

THE STARS

ZINEDINE ZIDANE

One the greatest players of his generation, and with a claim for best of all time, Zizou revelled in a World Cup held in his native country. 1998 was his first World Cup and he certainly made a mark, leading the French team to an opening win over Denmark before a red card against Saudi Arabia derailed his tournament. However, upon his return he was instrumental in getting France to the final, where his two goals sealed the nation's first ever World Cup win.

RONALDO

Winner of the tournament's Golden Ball, Ronaldo went into France '98 considered the world's best striker, and came out of it with that label fully intact. Four goals and three assists, including vital strikes against Chile and the Netherlands, helped Brazil reach the World Cup final. Only his mysterious pre-match illness in the tournament's showpiece blotted a perfect finals for the Brazilian sensation.

ZINEDINE ZIDANE

15

VIDEO GAMES

SUPER KICK OFF

A popular series from the very start of the decade, *Kick Off* had been a well-received title when it was released in 1989 and the early sequels that followed continued the same trend. There were five more Kick Off games in the 1990s, with *Super Kick Off* perhaps being the biggest title of the series. It was available across both the big Sega and Nintendo consoles, with the Mega Drive version a number one seller in 1991.

EUROPEAN CLUB SOCCER

A 1992 release for Sega Mega Drive, *European Club Soccer* pre-dates FIFA's and ISS' games and had a unique concept. Instead of national teams, this Virgin Games title concentrated solely on domestic leagues and each country was represented by at least two teams. In addition, the game also had correct club names and imitations of club badges, although real names were a step too far and were instead merged names of players within the squads.

SENSIBLE SOCCER

The most popular football game of the early 1990s, *Sensible Soccer* and their big heads still holds retro value in 2013. Look at it now and you may wonder how the game caused so much fuss; taken from a birdseye view – the first football game to use that type of camera angle – the rudimentary little men had little animation and larger than life heads, but were still capable of scoring spectacular goals. Yet at its core was a vastly addictive and simple

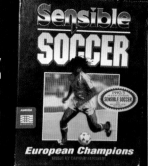

'90s MOMENT

Ruud Gullit became the first non-British manager to win a major trophy in England, when he led Chelsea to FA Cup victory in 1997.

football game whether you were playing it on the Amiga, Atari or Sega Mega Drive.
First released in 1992, the series went through a number of variations, including 1994's popular *Sensible World of Soccer*. The Amiga version was even re-released on the Xbox platform in 2007, in a full retro throwback of football games.

WORLD CUP ITALIA 90

The first video game themed around an actual World Cup finals, Sega's *World Cup Italia 90* was actually one of three Italia '90 games (along with *Italy 90 Soccer and Italia 1990* from Codemasters) but is the one remembered most fondly. Available on the Mega Drive and Master System formats, the game followed on from previous release, *World Cup Carnival*, with gameplay taken from a birdseye view of the pitch. Never the easiest game to score a goal on, it did feature all of the logos and mascot from Italia '90, and when you did manage to find the net there was a separate celebration graphic. It later became part of the *Mega Games* series, alongside famous Mega Drive titles *Super Hang On* and *Columns*.

World Cup Italia 90 sparked a trend that saw game releases for every major tournament of the 1990s. Elite's *European Championship 1992*, was followed by US Gold's *World Cup USA 94*, then Gremlin modified their Actua Soccer title for the release of *UEFA Euro 1996*. Finally, EA Sports revolutionised the line by incorporating their FIFA title into *World Cup 98*, which became the first World Cup game to use a 3D engine, and the most lifelike title thus far.

FIFA INTERNATIONAL SOCCER

The game-changer in football sims, EA Sports' much billed game *FIFA International Soccer* hit stores in July 1993, bearing the image of England's David Platt on its cover. The title broke with traditional 16-bit era games, and was presented in an isometric view rather than the more common top-down, side or birdseye view used in other football games of the time. Firing up the game the first thing you heard was 'EA Sports, it's in the game' which although a little strange made the title fresh and exciting. It featured only international teams, and fictional player names which meant hoping that Ken Law did the business for England in whatever mode you chose. Fond quirks of the games included a pre-match coin toss choosing, goalies that seemed to hold onto whatever type of shot you threw at them, and a range of goal celebrations that went as far as a re-enactment of a rocket launch on the screen. If you really wanted to get good at the game, you'd pick to play against Qatar, who were as leaky as a 1993 Swindon Town defence. While scoring goals became easier once you realised you could stand in front of the goalkeeper and watch his kick rebound off you into the net. And who could forget the EA All Stars team, now they were an unbeatable force.

The title was a big success, knocking *Street Fighter II* off the top of the charts, and led to EA Sports releasing a new version of the game every year. *FIFA 95* featured Erik Thorstvedt on the cover and included club teams for the first time, a year later real player names were featured for the first time, and by the end of the decade David Ginola, David Beckham and Dennis Bergkamp had all graced the cover, while the graphics had become less cartoon like and more

INTERNATIONAL SUPERSTAR SOCCER

Born in Japan, where it's more commonly known as *Winning Eleven*, Konami's *International Superstar Soccer* was one step ahead of its game rivals upon release in 1994. *ISS* made its debut exclusively on the Super Nintendo system, with a whole host of features that had yet to be seen on any football game, including what would later become its ultimate rival, *FIFA International Soccer*. Its lifelike approach meant numbers on the

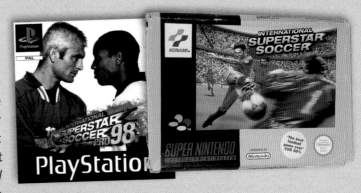

back of shirts for the first time, players who had distinctive features and diversities away from different shades of hair colour and looked like players of the time, and a commentator's voice for goals and other decisions. The game also had a more authentic look about it, shying away from the more cartoon-like approach seen from other console football titles around, and making it feel more like an arcade game. An approach that saw the game become the preferred choice of many football fans by the end of the decade, despite its lack of licenses for real player names and clubs. Instead, clever amalgamations were made so you could identify each star, like Roberto Larcos (Roberto Carlos), Juan Revon (Juan Veron) and Backham.

Konami released the game on Mega Drive in 1995, and later the Nintendo 64, Saturn and PlayStation while cover stars included Carlos Valderrama, Fabrizio Ravenelli and Paul Ince. That was until 2003, when the line was discontinued so the publishers could concentrate on new series *Pro Evolution Soccer*, to turn up the heat on rivals EA Sports and their *FIFA* title.

'90s MOMENT

Ravenelli was a £7 million signing for Middlesbrough in 1996, but the flamboyant Italian striker nicknamed 'The White Feather' couldn't prevent the club being relegated AND losing in both cup finals.

CHAMPIONSHIP MANAGER

If you've ever sat in front of a computer and suddenly realised you've let six hours pass without moving from your seat, one would assume that you were, like many of us in the 1990s, under the spell of one game, *Championship Manager*. An addiction so great it has ended relationships, prevented promotions, and been the real reason for late homework, everyone has been drawn into its world. The brainchild of brothers Paul and Ov Collyer, the pair came developed the game from their Shropshire bedrooms in the 1980s, calling it *European Champions*. Realising the potential in the game, it was bought by Domark right at the start of the decade and first released under the name *Championship Manager* in 1992. Sales were steady enough to grant the game a sequel a year later, this time with the added bonus of real-life player database – with Danny Murphy and Neil Lennon sitting in Crewe's reserve team just waiting to be picked up! This release really captured the football audience, and the game quickly built up a large following who were taken by the game's deep database. By 1995's *Championship Manager 2*, the success of the franchise went into overdrive, with a whole host of new features added including, for the first time, the in-match commentary engine that has now become synonymous with the game. From that point on its annual release was top of every football fan's wish list, and unearthed classic *Champs* players such as Kennedy Bakircioglü, Tonton Zola Moukoko and Nii Lamptey, who all became more famous for their talents in the game than they ever really did on an actual football pitch. Its popularity soared into the next decade, and under its current branding of *Football Manager* remains the most eagerly anticipated release of the season.

Champs wasn't the only manager game to have tickled our tactical brains during this era, there were quite a few competitors both before and after the rise of *Championship Manager*. *Player Manager* was perhaps the first real game of its ilk, first released for the Amiga system in 1990. And there have been a number of other similar management based titles including *1st Division Manager*, *1–0 Soccer Manager*, *Premier League Football Manager* and *LMA Manager*.

1992's *Premier Manager* has remained a near rival to *Championship Manager*, with its first release actually better received by gaming critics. Despite it being eventually overtaken in sales, it remained a popular game throughout the decade and is still releasing annual updates in today's market.

PLAYER ENDORSED

Games developers have been quick to cash in on player popularity over the years, and has seen some well-known faces endorse video games bearing their name. In the 1980s, Emlyn Hughes, Gary Lineker and Kenny Dalglish began the trend, and with the explosion of football and Italia '90 at the beginning of the decade, it gave publishers the opportunity to add a real-life touch to their games. Gascoigne continued his foray into the market with *Gazza II*, while there was also *John Barnes European Football Challenge* and *Graeme Souness International Soccer* released in 1992 as well as *Graham Taylor's England Manager*. The decade ended with *Michael Owen World League Soccer 99*, a PlayStation release by Eidos.

'90s MOMENT

As manager of Galatasaray in 1995, Graeme Souness sparked outrage when he planted a large club flag into the centre circle of arch rivals Fenerbahce's pitch. The gesture almost caused a full-blown riot, but earned him cult status among the Galatasaray fans.

IN THE ARCADE

It wasn't just at home that you could get your footballing game kicks, the arcades also had their fair share of footy titles too. Easily the best loved was *Virtua Striker*, a Sega game that first appeared in arcades in 1994. The first real 3D motion-graphic game, its rapid gameplay and smooth movements made it an essential stop when visiting arcades in the airport or on holiday – even its transition to console never really felt the same. Other arcade titles of the era include *Football Champ*, *Neo Geo Cup 98*, *Dream World Soccer* and *Goal! Goal! Goal!*.

WORTH A MENTION

With the rise of home computers and consoles in the 1990s, it's astonishing how many different football games were released in this decade. Whether it was Amiga or Amstrad, Mega Drive or SNES, or even Jaguar or PlayStation, we simply couldn't get enough of footy-based sims. So if I haven't already mentioned your favourite game, it might be among this list of alternatives.

Action Soccer, Actua Soccer, Champions of Europe, Complete Onside Soccer ,Dino Dinis Soccer, European Soccer Challenge, Fever Pitch, Football Champ, Football Glory, Goal, Marko's Magic Football, Mega Man Soccer, Olympic Soccer, Sega Worldwide Soccer 97, Soccer Mania, Striker, Super Match Soccer, Super Soccer Kid, Super Soccer, This Is Football, Total Football, Ultimate Soccer, World Soccer

16

READING

FEVER PITCH

Football books were something of a rarity before the 1990s, with publishers deeming football fans the type of audience they were unwilling to invest in. However, with the explosion of football over the decade, especially after England's success at Italia '90, it turned the tide when it came to the written word, and no book had a bigger influence than Nick Hornby's *Fever Pitch*.

Published in 1992, the book is an autobiographical tale of Hornby's love of Arsenal from the 1960s through to the 1990s. In it the writer's life is told not in years, but in seasons, and not by your standard daily calendar but by the Gunners' fixture list. It is an account of what being a football supporter really means, and the rollercoaster ride that goes with it. How your club becomes not just a football team, but a friend, a partner and a commitment for life. The highs, the lows, the love, the hate, the being selfish and being unreasonable, and how one defeat feels like a ripple effect intrinsically linked to your own life and fortunes. And for many,

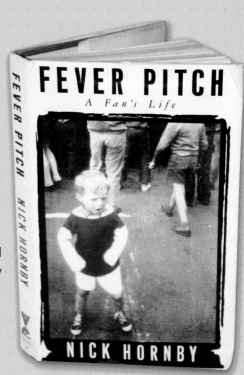

it hit home like no other piece of literature had before, a fellow fan who understood the pleasure and perils of being a football fan simply because he was one of them – and just so happened to be a brilliant writer too. It was Hornby's feelings put down on paper that made *Fever Pitch* such a major success, winning the William Hill Sports Book of the Year for 1992, and eventually selling over a million copies in the UK alone.

It is also often suggested that the book crossed the divide in terms of class and, thanks to Hornby's way with words, opened up a new audience to football in a way they hadn't viewed it before. This is something which Hornby has often dismissed, but it did give publishers reason to believe books about football were something they could now get behind. It seems a little too easy to claim *Fever Pitch* was entirely responsible for a new 'class' of football fan, and a little insulting to supporters who predate the book. However, it did open the minds and the market on both ends of the spectrum and paved the way for a genre that is now the norm in 2013. Twenty years on, the book is still being read by new generations and its timeless emotions given new leases of life.

In 1997, Hornby wrote a screenplay adaption for a film version of *Fever Pitch*. Starring Colin Firth as Paul Ashworth, the movie concentrated on Arsenal's 1988/89 First Division championship-winning season and the effect of the protagonist's life in and around Highbury. Focusing on Ashworth's romantic relationship with Sarah Hughes (played by Ruth Gemmell) and culminating in Arsenal's last-minute title-winning victory at Anfield. It was later remade into a Hollywood film by the Farrelly Brothers, switching the focus from football and Arsenal to baseball and the Boston Red Sox. Starring Jimmy Fallon and Drew Barrymore, it was renamed *The Perfect Catch* and released in 2005 to a lukewarm reception.

'90s MOMENT

One of the 1990s' most unusual moments occured at Highbury. While working on the ground to meet the new rules of the Taylor Report, Arsenal installed a mural of supporters on the North Bank to prevent fans seeing the building works.

ANNUALS

Christmas Day was usually full of these treats under the tree, an obvious buy for football fans - the obligatory football annual. Whether it be the spin off from your favourite magazine, like *Match* or *Shoot*, or titles themed around TV shows *Match of the Day* and ITV's *The Match*, the festive holiday was spent perusing these annuals, which were for all intents and purposes 'best ofs' from the product's past year. Puzzles, posters and reviews were the standard format, and were essential to anyone's bookshelf in this decade.

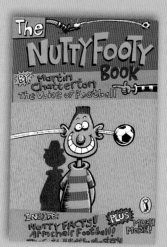

WORTH A MENTION

Fever Pitch's success meant there was more scope for football titles and there were a few notable titles published during the decade. Football hooliganism was the theme for both Kevin Sampson's **Awaydays** and John King's **The Football Factory**, the latter being made into a 2004 film. Simon Kuper's **Football Against The Enemy** was published to acclaim in 1994, as he travelled across twenty-two different countries to examine the way football had shaped them. Pete Davies' account of the 1990 World Cup **All Played Out** is also worth a read.

MORE MOMENTS

FIRST BATTLE OF OLD TRAFFORD

20 October 1991

Manchester United and Arsenal were battling on the field long before flying pizzas and Martin Keown hairdryers. This clash in 1991 involved twenty-one of the twenty-two outfield players and saw both teams docked points for their actions.

JURGEN DIVES INTO ENGLAND

13 August 1994

A major coup for Spurs, Jürgen Kilnsmann arrived at White Hart Lane in the summer of 1994 to a stellar reputation of goalscoring, but a somewhat questionable one for his diving. All that was quickly squashed with two goals on his debut and a celebration to mock such suggestions.

CANTONA'S CROWD CONTROL

25 January 1995
King Eric pushed the boundaries when it came to the term 'maverick' and no further than this personal take on stewarding at Selhurst Park. The kung-fu kick on a Crystal Palace fan earned the Frenchman a nine-month ban from the game.

THE SCORPION KICK

6 September 1995
If it hadn't been for René Higuita there wouldn't have been much to write home about this goalless draw between England and Colombia. One 'scorpion kick' save from Jamie Redknapp later and every young fan was going to bed determined to re-enact the move next time they were on the pitch.

THE BEST PREMIER LEAGUE GAME

3 April 1996
Seen over and over again, the clash between Liverpool and Newcastle at Anfield is widely considered as the Premier League's greatest ever game. With Newcastle's title bid faltering, Kevin Keegan took his troops to his old stomping ground, where in a brilliantly topsy-turvy match the Magpies lost to a ninety-second minute Stan Collymore strike, losing 4–3. Epic.

TITO BURIES BARCA

18 September 1997

Faustino Asprilla didn't have many nights as the Toon Army's hero, but this one will remain in Geordie hearts forever. The Colombian's hat-trick sunk the Catalan giants, Rivaldo, Figo and all, and his corner-flag celebration remains a St James' Park fave.

PAULO'S RED MIST

24 October 1998

Another maverick involved in his own battle against authority. Not happy with the decision to send him off in this clash with Arsenal in 1998, Sheffield Wednesday's Paulo Di Canio took it out on ref Paul Alcock with a gentle shove that turned into a comedy fall from the man in black.

RAISE A GLASS FOR JIMMY

8 May 1999

What better way to end than with a true fairytale story. It's the last minute of the last game of the season and Carlisle are about to be relegated out of the Football League. One goal from on-loan keeper Jimmy Glass later, and his name in United folklore is secured forever.

NOT FORGETTING

CLUBCALL

Before the internet there was only one sure-fire way to find out the latest football news from your club. Unfortunately it meant racking up a horrendously large phone bill to do so. Clubcall came about in 1986 and was at its peak during the 1990s, when it was the go-to guide to all that was happening at your favourite club. All league clubs had their own line and would provide interviews with the players, transfer news and big game previews – all for a premium rate phone call price, which Dad wouldn't be happy with. What made it worse was the tempting, yet usually completely made up headlines that ran across Teletext, urging and leaving you with no other choice to call and find out the full story. Which was almost always a let down.

NUTS

A quirky piece of 1990s, well, tat really, that I still have sitting on my desk at home. If you were 'nuts' about football, then your life clearly wasn't complete without a china-made walnut with smiling face and obligatory football kit. Mine obviously wasn't, as I own three different versions of the unusual ornament.

WINDOW BANNERS

Making sure the world knows who you support is an important part of being a football fan, so no bedroom window was free of these novelty window hangers in this era, or any era since. Whether it be your team's kit, some amusing satire of your rivals or the most common one, the 'I'd rather be watching …' window decoration. Found in club stores, and for some reason in seaside shops around beach resorts, usually outside on a rotating shelf and next to the iron-on team transfers and porcelain gnomes.

CLUB MEMBERSHIPS

There was no better way of feeling like you were part of a football club than being part of its membership club. For a small percentage of your monthly pocket money, your membership would include free gifts upon joining, greeting cards on your birthday and Christmas and regular newsletters throughout the season.

HAPPY MEALS

Kids have never needed much persuasion for a trip to McDonald's, especially given the treats the fast food chain would add to their well-presented Happy Meals every month. When they weren't giving away toys of fries that turned into robots or their mascot riding a racecar, McDonald's managed to tap into the football fever surrounding major tournaments with Happy Meals and toys dedicated to the events. You may have already spotted the products in the book somewhere, but here are the full sets for both World Cup '94 and '98. Did you manage to collect them all?

ACKNOWLEDGEMENTS

There are a number of people I would like to thank for making this book possible, and to say how humbled I was by their co-operation during my 1990s nostalgia trip.

Firstly to Liam Sheppard, who was responsible for the majority of the shots in this book. Your time and patience with me and the hundreds of images was vital in making this book possible. To Richard Leatherdale, Paul Baillie-Lane, Rowena Williams and everyone at The History Press for believing in this title and the era as much as I did, including Martin Latham for the cover design and Chris West for the internal design. To friends, family and colleagues for their own memories of the decade that helped me along – especially Joe Chilvers, Peter Hunt and the Credit Suisse gang, along with the Loft For Words message board and Rob Gallagher's important mementos. To my Mum and Dad for being kind enough to spoil me with football stuff in the 1990s, and for letting me store them in their loft for all these years. To Jackie Gallagher, for becoming a 90s expert thanks to her subbing.

To Billy Robertson at Action Images, for once again providing the action shots needed and always being on hand for important queries, and Sarah Spalding at the *Evening Standard* for her advice and images. To Alex Henderson at Sky Sports for his willingness and images that really helped the book. Greg Double and Tom Burrow at Umbro, for giving us so much material, unfortunately we couldn't use it all – as hard as I tried. To Ryan Greenwood at Nike for his persistence and belief in the title, and for getting me exactly what I needed. Ben Goldhagen for making sure we could show Adidas' role in the decade, and to Dom D'Altilla for literally digging out as much as he could find from the Topps archive. The following people also deserve a massive thank you for their help, your kindness was immensely appreciated:

James Davids (Warner); Barry Hughes and Viki Elmer (Corinthians); Kyri Demetriou (Mitre); Colin Mitchell and Daniel Tyler (*Shoot*); James Bandy (*Match*); Thomas Barnsley (McDonald's); Edward Whitehead, Stacey Pinkus and Lucy Hawe (Pizza Hut); Stuart Davis (Walkers); Francesca Scott (*Hurricanes*); Tom Spiers (Gamesdatabase); Philip Skelland (Zeon); Chris Carlin (Upper Deck); Andy Lyons and Doug Cheeseman (*When Saturday Comes*); Natalie House (Nickelodeon); Keith Hennessey and Shaun White (EA); Ben Harper (Magic Box); Liz Barnes and Stuart Anderton (*Total Football*); Richard Walker and Ben Young (Fabulous Films); Poppy North (Penguin); Fiona Smith (Hamlyn); Jane Slatter; Fiona Hortopp (Top Trumps); Nick Mouton (Hasbro); Kirsty Scott (Tomy); Sarah King (IPC Publishing); Doug at Classic Football Shirts; Steve Merrett (Konami); Maddie at Coca-Cola; Martin Combeer, Gemma Oakes, Alison Day, Gary Dixon and Nick Rodgerson (Puma); Selina Dangerfield (Vivid); Jessica Doran and Stefano Melegari (Panini); Joanna Franks (Immediate); Iain Macintosh; Jessica Noon (Kellog's); Ben Blanco; Roy Meredith (Eidos); Jason Christian (Teletext); Samira Agamasu (EMI); Sarah Head (Sega); Mark Watson; Abbie Dando (Golden Wonder); Rich Eddy (Codemasters); Jamie Sefton; Ben Smith (News International); Katy Williams; John Packard and Melanie Leggett (Egmont); Ian Stewart; Glen Holland (Adidas); Sebastian Bell; Emma Rule and Daisy Sheppard (Wash 'n' Go); Bethany Henry (L'Oreal); James Mills (Channel 4); Kate Seamark (Nestle); Claire Feeney (All3 Media); Steve Gulbis; Melanie Waite-Johnston (Unilever); David Halls (*FourFourTwo*); Andy McConachie (Footballcardsuk.com); Anna Gibson (Advertising Agency); Stephen Morgan (Midas); Miles Jacobson (SI Games); Martyn McFadden and Paul (A Love Supreme); Nick Barrett and Roger White (NorthoneTV); Mike Wade; Adam Merrett (Capcom); Ashley Westgate (Zeppelin); Phil Watkins (The Football Pools); Sina Haug and Paul Sherratt (Uhlsport); Ann Skovrider (Hummel); Mike Harrison (*The City Gent*); Sam at Mondelez; Steve Ryan and Andrew Wainstein (Fantasy League); Hope Hadfield (Burtons Biscuits); Tom Hodson and Kevin Morgan (ITV); Helen at Kidsera; Richard Holt (Press Association).

Finally a big thank you to Jo, for her ongoing love, photography expertise and patience putting up with a house full of classic mementoes (or any of the other words she may have called it).

PICTURE CREDITS